T0285521

THE ROYAL COURT THEATRE PRESENTS

two Palestinians
go dogging

by Sami Ibrahim

In partnership with Theatre Uncut

two Palestinians go dogging was first performed at the Royal Court
Jerwood Theatre Upstairs, Sloane Square, on Saturday 7 May 2022.

two Palestinians go dogging
by Sami Ibrahim

CAST (in alphabetical order)

Jawad **Luca Kamleh Chapman**
Salwa **Sofia Danu**
Tariq **Joe Haddad**
Adam **Philipp Mogilnitskiy**
Reem **Hala Omran**
Sara **Mai Weisz**
Sayeed **Miltos Yerolemou**

Director **Omar Elerian**
Designer **Rajha Shakiry**
Associate Designer **Ruth Hall**
Lighting Designer **Jackie Shemesh**
Sound Designer **Elena Peña**
Video Designer **Zakk Hein**
Assistant Director **Alessandra Davison**
Associate Lighting Designer **Lucía Sánchez Roldán**
Fight Director **Bret Yount**
Stage Managers **Rike Berg, Evelin Thomas**
Stage Management Work Placement **Lottie Denby**
Set built by **Royal Court Stage Department, Ridiculous Solutions &
Weldfab Stage Engineering**

From the Royal Court, on this production:

Casting Directors **Amy Ball & Arthur Carrington**
Company Manager **Joni Carter**
Stage Supervisor **TJ Chappell-Meade**
Lighting and Video Supervisor **Max Cherry**
Production Manager **Simon Evans**
Lead Producer **Chris James**
Costume Supervisor **Katie Price**

The Royal Court & Stage Management wish to thank the following for their help with this production:
Young Vic Theatre, The Toy Project, Queen's Theatre Hornchurch,
Lucy White (costume placement)

two Palestinians go dogging

by Sami Ibrahim

Sami Ibrahim (Writer)

Theatre includes: **Metamorphoses (Globe); Wonder Winterland (Oxford School of Drama/Soho); Wind Bit Bitter, Bit Bit Bit Her (VAULT Festival); the Palestinian in the basement is on fire (Pint Sized/Bunker); Iron Dome Fog Dome (First Drafts, Yard); Force of Trump (Theatre N16/The Space/Brockley Jack); Carnivore (Write Now 7 Festival, Brockley Jack).**

Awards include: **Theatre Uncut Political Playwriting Award.**

Sami has been writer-in-residence at the Globe and one of the Genesis Almeida New Playwrights. He has been on attachment at the National Theatre Studio and Theatr Clwyd, and a member of the Tamasha Writers Group and Oxford Playhouse Playmaker programme.

Rike Berg (Stage Manager-book)

For the Royal Court: **The Song Project, Living Newspaper.**

Other theatre includes: **The Woman in Black (& Sweden tour), Belongings (Gothenburg English Studio Theatre); Upper Cut, Working–The Musical (Southwark); Lines (Yard); Sense of an Ending, Clickbait, Four Play, We Wait In Joyful Hope, The Monkey, Years of Sunlight, Burning Bridges (Theatre503); Fury (Soho); These Trees Are Made of Blood (Arcola); Contractions (Deafinitely Theatre); Misty, Nine Night (West End); Strange Fruit, The Arrival, Overflow (Bush); Love and Other Acts of Violence (Donmar); The Chairs (Almeida).**

Opera includes: **Isabeau (Opera Holland Park).**

Rike has also worked for the Royal Albert Hall, Assembly, Pleasance, Complicité, Breach, Gate, Scene & Heard, NYT, Polka, Stratford East, Hampstead and Young Vic.

Sofia Danu (Salwa)

Theatre includes: **A Land Without Jasmine (BAC/Sarha Collective); Kan Ya Makan (Riyadh); Ellipsis (Rose Company); Salome (Space); Today Is My 100th Birthday (Edinburgh Festival Fringe); Battle Cry (Apiary Studios); Now Here & In Between (Al-Balad, Jordan).**

Television includes: **Moon Knight, Silent Witness, The Citadel Folks, Shawq.**

Film includes: **The Way of the Wind, Held For Ransom, Fay's Palette, Moderately Satisfied (Short).**

Radio includes: **Yarmouk, Decolonising History.**

Alessandra Davison (Assistant Director)

As director, theatre includes: **Three Sisters (Lyric, Hammersmith); Call Me Maybe (Arcola); Moving In/On (The Bunker); Hatch (Baron's Court); By Way of Kensal Green (Theatre503).**

As co-director, theatre includes: **Drylands (Tramshed).**

As assistant & associate director, theatre includes: **A Number (Old Vic); Idyll (Pentabus); Torch Song (Turbine); Me for the World (Young Vic); CARE (The PappyShow).**

Digital includes: **SWAY (Virtual Collaborators).**

Alessandra is a director, photographer and dramaturg. She is currently a director in the Jamie Lloyd EMERGE company, a reader for Park Theatre and a committee member of Stage Sight. She recently underwent dramaturgy training on the Paines Plough Re:Assemble professional development programme.

Omar Elerian (Director)

As director, theatre includes: **The Chairs (Almeida); Autoreverse (BAC); Going Through, Misty, NASSIM, One Cold Dark Night, Islands (Bush).**

As co-director, theatre includes: **The Mill: City of Dreams (site-specific); You're Not Like The Other Girls Chrissy (China Plate).**

As associate director, theatre includes: **Leave Taking, The Royale, Perseverance Drive, Chalet Lines (Bush).**

Omar was the Resident Associate Director at the Bush Theatre 2012-2018.

Joe Haddad (Tariq)

Theatre includes: **The Jumper Factory (Young Vic/HOME, Manchester); For the Living (Talos Festival/Bread & Roses); Nazanin's Story (Edinburgh Festival Fringe/Barbican/Tour).**

Television includes: **Danny Boy.**

Radio includes: **Yarmouk.**

Film includes: **London Tomorrow [short].**

Ruth Hall (Associate Designer)

As designer, theatre includes: **Sydney and the Old Girl (The Park Theatre); The Permanent Way (Vaults); The Caucasian Chalk Circle (Theatr Genedlaethol); Anna Karenina (East 15); Sonny (ArtsEd); 46 Beacon (Trafalgar Studios); Macbeth (Caerphilly Castle); Blackbird (TOR); Play Strindberg (Ustinov); Contractions (Chapter Arts Centre); Fijiland (Southwark); Little Shop of Horrors, Salt, Root and Roe, (Theatr Clwyd); Noah (Chichester); The Road To Mecca (Arcola).**

As associate designer, theatre includes: **Home I'm Darling (National/Theatr Clwyd); The Writer (Almeida); Crime and Punishment, A Streetcar Named Desire (Theatre Cocoon, Tokyo); Shakespeare in Love (Bath Theatre Royal); Mystery Plays (York Minster); Of Mice and Men (West Yorkshire Playhouse); London Road (National); Zorro (Garrick); The Comedy of Errors, The Hypocrite, Shoemakers Holiday, Henry VI Trilogy, Romeo and Juliet, The Tempest, The Winter's Tale and Pericles (RSC).**

As art department assistant, film includes: **- London Road, Cuba Pictures, 2014.**

Zakk Hein (Video Designer)

As video designer, theatre includes: **Secret Life of Humans (New Diorama/tour); Occupational Hazards (Hampstead); Looking Through Glass, The Mountaintop (The Other Room); A Good Clean Heart (Wales Millennium Centre/tour); Swansea's Three Night Blitz (Grand, Swansea); Saturday Night Forever (Aberystwyth Arts Centre, tour).**

As video designer, opera includes: **Ariodante (Royal College of Music); Pelléas et Mélisande, The Tales of Hoffmann (English Touring Opera/tour).**

As associate video designer, theatre includes: **Desire Under the Elms (Crucible, Sheffield); Ugly Lies the Bone (National); Alice's Adventures Underground (Les Enfants Terribles).**

Luca Kamleh Chapman (Jawad)

two Palestinians go dogging is Luca's professional debut.

Philipp Mogilnitskiy (Adam)

Theatre includes: **Iran Conference (Weda, Warsaw); The Trials of John Demjanjuk: A Holocaust Cabaret (Confrontation/NET Festivals); The Face of Jizo (Ethud); Brothers & Sisters, An Enemy of the People, Gaudeamus, Life & Fate, Our Class, Blue Light (Maly Drama, St. Petersburg); The Pillowman, Time to be Ashes (On Theatre, St. Petersburg).**

Television includes: **House under Two Eagles, Into The Night (Israel), Król, S'parta, Ziuk: The Young Pilsudski, De 12 Van Schouwendam, Maly Zgon, Nielegalni, Podkidysh, Ulyotnyy Ekipazh, Full Moon, Ne Vmeste, Takaya Rabota.**

Film includes: **MINSK, Zatopek, What the French Keep Still About.**

Hala Omran (Reem)

Theatre includes: **I Medea, In The Eruptive Mode, UR (SABAB, Kuwait/International tours); 72 Virgins, UR 2, X Adra, Oh You, Whom I Love, The Juste, Romeo & Juliet, Andromache (International tours); The Poem, Land of the Arab Language 1, 2 & 3 (Odéon Théâtre de l'Europe); A Streetcar Named Desire (Syrian National Theatre); The Seagull (Damascus).**

Dance includes: **As Told By My Mother, Night, May He Rise & Smell The Fragrance (Zukak, Beirut/International tours).**

Opera includes: **Kalila & Dimna (Aix-en-Provence Festival).**

Film includes: **Romeo & Juliet, Dreamy Vision, Under the Ceiling, The Gate to the Sun, The Box of Life.**

Awards include: **Journées Théatrales de Carthage Best Actress Award (I Medea); Cairo International Festival for Experimental Theatre Best Actress Award (I Medea).**

Elena Peña (Sound Designer)

For the Royal Court: **Maryland, seven methods of killing kylie jenner, Living Newspaper.**

Other theatre includes: **The Chairs, Mass Observation (Almeida); Trouble in Mind (National); Nora: A Doll's House, Rockets & Blue Lights (& National), Macbeth, Mountains (Royal Exchange, Manchester); Autoreverse (BAC); Brainstorm (Company Three/National); Reasons You Should(n't) Love Me, Snowflake, The Kilburn Passion, Arabian Nights (Kiln); Misty (& West End), Going Through, Hir, Islands (Bush); The Memory of Water (Nottingham Playhouse); The Remains of the Day (Out of Joint/Royal Derngate, Northampton); Thick As Thieves (Clean Break/Clwyd); All of Me (China Plate); Double Vision (Wales Millennium Centre); The Caretaker (Bristol Old Vic).**

Dance includes: **Patrias, Quimeras (Sadlers Wells/Paco Peña Flamenco Company).**

Radio includes: **Rockets & Blue Lights, The Meet Cute, Twelve Years, Duchamps Urinal.**

Installation includes: **Have Your Circumstances Changed?, Yes These Eyes Are The Windows (ArtAngel).**

Lucía Sánchez Roldán
(Associate Lighting Designer)

As lighting designer, theatre includes: **Tapped (Theatre 503); The Forest Awakens, Code and Dagger, A New Beginning (Kiln); The Gift (GBS RADA); Barbarians (Silk Street); Everything Must Go (Playground); Invisibles, The First (VAULT Festival); The Spirit (BAC); Ms Julie, Utopia Room (The Place); The Niceties (Finborough); How We Begin (Kings Head).**

As associate lighting designer, theatre includes: **Cabaret (Playhouse); Camp Siegfried (Old Vic); Taboo Anniversary Concert (London Palladium); Mirror and the Light (Gielgud); Amélie (Criterion); Les Misérables-The Staged Concert (Sondheim); Moonlight and Magnolias (Nottingham Playhouse); The Fishermen (West End/Marlowe).**

Rajha Shakiry (Designer)

For the Royal Court: **seven methods of killing kylie jenner.**

Other theatre includes: **Trouble in Mind, Nine Night (& West End), Master Harold & the Boys (National); The Mountaintop (Young Vic/UK tour/Royal Exchange, Manchester); Return of Danton (Collective Ma'louba, Germany); Autoreverse (BAC); Richard II (Globe); Misty (& West End), Going Through (Bush); The Dark (Fuel); Muhammad Ali & Me (Albany & UK tour); Mobile (Paper Birds); How Nigeria Became (Unicorn); Sweet Taboo (Embassy); I Stand Corrected (Artscape/Ovalhouse); Richard II (Ashtar/Hisham's Palace/Jericho/Globe); Still Life Dreaming (Pleasance, Edinburgh); Safe (New Diorama); The Lion & the Unicorn (Eastern Angles); Krunch (National Arts Festival, Grahamstown); Speak (Albany/Rich Mix); Moj of the Antartic (Lyric, Hammersmith/Ovalhouse/South Africa tour); Visible (Contact, Manchester/Liverpool Everyman/Ustinov, Bath/Soho); Everything is Illuminated, Nymphs & Shepherds (Ectetera); Goblin Market (Sydmonton Festival/Southwark); The Ghost Downstairs [co-designer] (New Perspectives); The Wall, Changes (Cardboard Citizens).**

Dance includes: **Head Wrap Diaries (The Place); Power Games (Jerwood Dance, Ipswich/Edinburgh Festival Fringe).**

Opera includes: **Don Giovanni, Le Nozze Di Figaro (St Andrew's Church/Beauforthuis, Netherlands).**

Rajha's work was exhibited at the V&A's Make: Believe Exhibition.

Jackie Shemesh (Lighting Designer)

Theatre includes: **The Chairs, Mary Stuart (&West End), Vanya (Almeida); White Noise (Bridge); Changing Destiny, In the Penal Colony, Man, Oh My Sweet Land (Young Vic); The Return of Danton (Mulheim Theatre); The Seagull (West End); Death of England: Delroy, Death of England, Hansard, (National); The Half God of Rainfall (Birmingham Rep/Kiln); The Audience (Nuffield, Southampton); Misty (& West End), The Beloved, Islands (Bush); What if Women Ruled the World?, Ceremony (Manchester International Festival).**

Dance includes: **Aftermath, Run Mary Run (Sadler's Wells); Goat (Rambert); Juliet & Romeo, Paradise Lost, It Needs Horses (Lost Dog); American Boy, American Man (Hetain Patel); The Murmuring, Young Men (BalletBoyz); Beheld, Hot Mess, Let's Talk About Dis (Candoco); Girl A (Scottish Dance); Lunatic (National Dance Company of Wales); Several works with dance artist Serafine 1369.**

Opera & orchestra includes: **Il Ritorno D'Ulisse in Patria (Grange Opera); Recital for Cathy, From Canyons to Stars (Hamburg Symphonic Orchestra); Sante (London Symphonic Orchestra).**

Performance: **This Unfortunate Thing Between Us [TUTBU TV], JRMIP (Hebbel-am-Ufer, Berlin).**

Evelin Thomas
(Stage Manager-Props)

As stage manager, theatre includes: **An Evening with the Good Enough Mum's Club (Birmingham Hippodrome); Oklahoma! (Momentum Performing Arts Academy, Bushey); Vernon God Little (Webber Douglas Studio, RCSSD).**

As assistant stage manager, theatre includes: **Much Ado About Nothing (RSC); The Witchfinder's Sister, Neville's Island (Queen's, Hornchurch); As You Like It (Public Acts Initiative, National); Two For The Seesaw (Buckland Theatre Company/West End).**

Mai Weisz (Sara)

Theatre includes: **On Cloud Nine (White Bear).**

Television includes: **This is Going to Hurt.**

Audio includes: **I'm Not Into Politics (Things I Am Not podcast/LegalAliens).**

Film includes: **Il n'y a pas d'ombre dans le desert.**

Miltos Yerolemou (Sayeed)

Theatre includes: **Young Marx (Bridge); King Lear, You Can't Take It With You, Animal Crackers (Royal Exchange, Manchester); Cyrano de Bergerac, Great Expectations, A Midsummer Night's Dream (& International tour), A Christmas Carol (Bristol Old Vic); The Lion, the Witch & the Wardrobe (Kensington Palace Gardens); One Flew Over the Cuckoo's Nest (Curve, Leicester); Adelaide Road, Twelfth Night, Othello, Beauty & the Beast, A Winter's Tale (RSC); Hansel & Gretel, Travels with My Aunt (Royal & Derngate, Northampton); The Comedy of Errors (Globe); Tintin (West End); Guys & Dolls (Donmar); Sleeping Beauty (Young Vic); The Misanthrope (Chichester Festival); Romeo & Juliet (Belgrade, Coventry).**

Opera includes: **A Midsummer Night's Dream (Aix Festival, France/Beijing).**

Television includes: **Dangerous Liaisons, Slow Horses, Becoming Elizabeth, The Crown, Game of Thrones, Wolf Hall, Critical, My Family, Black Books, Absolutely Fabulous.**

Film includes: **The Hitman's Wife's Bodyguard, Murder on the Orient Express, DJ, Star Wars – Episode VII: The Force Awakens, The Danish Girl, The Inbetweeners Movie.**

Bret Yount (Fight Director)

For the Royal Court: **The Glow, Cyprus Avenue (& Abbey, Dublin/Public, NYC), The Cane, X, Linda, Violence & Son, The Low Road, In Basildon, Wastwater, No Quarter, Belong, Remembrance Day, Redbud, Spur of the Moment, The Nether (& West End).**

Other theatre includes: **The Middle, The Normal Heart, Top Girls, Nine Night, Ma Rainey's Black Bottom, Treasure Island, A Taste of Honey, Emil & the Detectives, The World of Extreme Happiness, Double Feature, Moon on a Rainbow Shawl, Men Should Weep (National); City of Angels, Caroline or Change, Girl From the North Country, Foxfinder, Red Velvet, The Winter's Tale/Harlequinade, American Buffalo, Bad Jews, Fences, Posh, Absent Friends, Death & the Maiden, Clybourne Park, The Harder They Come, (West End); Richard III, Private Lives (UK tour); Hamlet, The Cherry Orcahrd (Theatre Royal, Windsor); The Winter's Tale (Cheek by Jowl); A Very Expensive Poison, Fanny & Alexander, The Hairy Ape (Old Vic); Nine Night, The Wasp (Trafalgar Studios); The One, Blueberry Toast, First Love is the Revolution (Soho); Hamlet (Barbican); Richard II, The Tempest, Much Ado About Nothing, Romeo & Juliet, Anne Boleyn (Globe); Medea (Gate); Tipping the Velvet (Lyric, Hammersmith); Much Ado About nothing, The Magician's Elephant, King Lear, The Merchant of Venice, Arden of Faversham, The Roaring Girl, Wolf Hall/Bring Up the Bodies, Candide (RSC); 'Tis Pity She's a Whore, The Broken Heart (Sam Wanamaker Playhouse); Force Majeure, Teenage Dick, Europe, Appropriate, Splendour, Roots, City of Angels, The Physicists, The Recruiting Officer (Donmar); The Trial, A Streetcar Named Desire, A Season in the Congo, Public Enemy (Young Vic); Ghosts (& Trafalgar Studios/BAM, NYC), Chimerica (& West End), Children's Children, The Knot of the Heart, House of Games, Ruined (Almeida); The Norman Conquests, A Streetcar Named Desire, Macbeth, The Caretaker, Lost Monsters (Liverpool Playhouse/Everyman, Liverpool); After the End, Dangerous Lady, Shalom, Baby, A Clockwork Orange – The Musical, The Graft, Two Women, Gladiator Games, Bashment (Theatre Royal, Stratford East).**

Television includes: **Quick Cuts, Against All Odds, Blue Peter.**

Film includes: **Troy.**

THE ROYAL COURT THEATRE

The Royal Court Theatre is the writers' theatre. It is a leading force in world theatre for cultivating and supporting writers – undiscovered, emerging and established.

Through the writers, the Royal Court is at the forefront of creating restless, alert, provocative theatre about now. We open our doors to the unheard voices and free thinkers that, through their writing, change our way of seeing.

Over 120,000 people visit the Royal Court in Sloane Square, London, each year and many thousands more see our work elsewhere through transfers to the West End and New York, UK and international tours, digital platforms, our residencies across London, and our site-specific work. Through all our work we strive to inspire audiences and influence future writers with radical thinking and provocative discussion.

The Royal Court's extensive development activity encompasses a diverse range of writers and artists and includes an ongoing programme of writers' attachments, readings, workshops and playwriting groups. Twenty years of the International Department's pioneering work around the world means the Royal Court has relationships with writers on every continent.

Since 1956 we have commissioned and produced hundreds of writers, from John Osborne to Jasmine Lee-Jones. Royal Court plays from every decade are now performed on stage and taught in classrooms and universities across the globe.

We're now working to the future and are committed to becoming a carbon net zero arts venue throughout 2020 to ensure we can continue to work for generations of writers and audiences to come.

It is because of this commitment to the writer and our future that we believe there is no more important theatre in the world than the Royal Court.

Find out more at royalcourttheatre.com

Supported using public funding by
ARTS COUNCIL ENGLAND

THEATRE UNCUT

Theatre Uncut creates bold, progressive, uncompromising political theatre.

We galvanise action, raise awareness and fuel debate by creating political new writing and making it available for everyone, everywhere.

We work with the world's leading playwrights and extraordinary new voices to create work that examines the world we live in today. We then make this work available for anyone to perform anywhere.

The company was created in 2011 to challenge the government's proposed cuts in public spending. Since then our work has explored subjects from austerity to the Arab Spring, from the Occupy movement to Black Lives Matter.

So far we have worked with 52 playwrights from 14 countries to create plays that have been performed by over 10,000 people in 32 countries across 4 continents, in schools, universities, theatres, village halls and on the streets. Our digital work has been watched by over 200,000 audience members online.

The Theatre Uncut Political Playwriting Award was created to discover and support the next generation of political playwrights in partnership with the Young Vic, Traverse Theatre, Sherman Theatre, Lyric Theatre Belfast, Independent Talent and Nick Hern Books.

Books Uncut was created to publish politically responsive writing for theatre and make the archive of Theatre Uncut plays available for people across the world to read, study and perform themselves.

We believe that theatre has the power to make positive social change.

ROYAL

ASSISTED PERFORMANCES

Captioned Performances

Captioned performances are accessible for people who are D/deaf, deafened & hard of hearing, as well as being suitable for people for whom English is not a first language.

two Palestinians go dogging: Fri 27 May, 7.45pm
That Is Not Who I Am: Wed 29 Jun, Wed 6 Jul, 7.30pm, Thu 14 Jul, 2.30pm

BSL-interpreted Performances

BSL-interpreted performances, delivered by an interpreter, give a sign interpretation of the text spoken and/or sung by artists in the onstage production.

That Is Not Who I Am: Wed 13 Jul, 7.30pm

Audio-described Performances

Audio-described performances are accessible for people who are blind or partially sighted. They are preceded by a touch tour which allows patrons access to elements of theatre design including set and costume.

That Is Not Who I Am: Sat 9 Jul, 2.30pm (Touch Tour at 1pm)

COURT

ROYAL

ASSISTED PERFORMANCES

Performances in a Relaxed Environment

Relaxed Environment performances are suitable for those who may benefit
from a more relaxed environment.

During these performances:

– There is a relaxed attitude to noise in the auditorium; you are welcome to
  respond to the show in whatever way feels natural
– You can enter and exit the auditorium when needed
– We will help you find the best seats for your experience
– House lights may remain raised slightly
– Loud noises may be reduced

two Palestinians go dogging: Sat 28 May, 3pm
That Is Not Who I Am: Sat 16 Jul, 2.30pm

If you would like to talk to us about your access requirements, please contact
our Box Office at (0)20 7565 5000 or boxoffice@royalcourttheatre.com
The Royal Court Visual Story is available on our website. Story and Sensory
synopses are available on the show pages via the Whats On tab of the
website shortly after Press Night.

COURT

ROYAL COURT SUPPORTERS

The Royal Court relies on its supporters in addition to our core grant from Arts Council England and our ticket sales. We are particularly grateful to the individuals, trusts and companies who stood by us and continued to support our work during these recent difficult times. It is with this vital support that the Royal Court remains the writers' theatre and that we can continue to seek out, develop and nurture new voices, both on and off our stages.

Thank you to all who support the Royal Court in this way. We really can't do it without you.

PUBLIC FUNDING

Supported using public funding by
**ARTS COUNCIL
ENGLAND**

CHARITABLE PARTNERS

BackstageTrust

**JERWOOD
ARTS**

ORANGE TREE
TRUST

CORPORATE SPONSORS

Aqua Financial Ltd
Cadogan
Colbert
Edwardian Hotels, London
SISTER

CORPORATE MEMBERS

Platinum
Auriens
Bloomberg Philanthropies

Silver
Left Bank Pictures
Patrizia
Sloane Stanley

TRUSTS & FOUNDATIONS

The Backstage Trust
Martin Bowley Charitable Trust
The City Bridge Trust
The Cleopatra Trust
Cockayne – Grants for the Arts
The Noël Coward Foundation
Cowley Charitable Foundation
The D'Oyly Carte Charitable Trust
Garrick Charitable Trust
The Golden Bottle Trust
Roderick & Elizabeth Jack
Jerwood Arts
Kirsh Foundation
The London Community Foundation
Clare McIntyre's Bursary
Old Possum's Practical Trust
Richard Radcliffe Charitable Trust
Rose Foundation
Royal Victoria Hall Foundation
The Charles Skey Charitable Trust
John Thaw Foundation
Thistle Trust
The Victoria Wood Foundation

**To find out more about supporting the Royal Court please get in touch
with the Development Team at support@royalcourttheatre.com, call
020 7565 5030 or visit royalcourttheatre.com/support-us**

ROYAL

BAR & KITCHEN

The Royal Court's Bar & Kitchen aims to create a welcoming and inspiring environment with a style and ethos that reflects the work we put on stage. Alongside our vibrant basement bar, you can visit our pop-up outdoor bar Court in the Square.

Offering expertly crafted cocktails alongside an extensive selection of craft gins and beers, wine and soft drinks, the Royal Court bars provide a sanctuary in the middle of Sloane Square. By day a perfect spot for meetings or quiet reflection and by night atmospheric meeting spaces for cast, crew, audiences and the general public.

All profits go directly to supporting the work of the Royal Court theatre, cultivating and supporting writers – undiscovered, emerging and established.

For more information, visit
royalcourttheatre.com/bar

HIRES & EVENTS

The Royal Court is available to hire for celebrations, rehearsals, meetings, filming, ceremonies and much more. Our two theatre spaces can be hired for conferences and showcases, and the building is a unique venue for bespoke events and receptions.

For more information, visit
royalcourttheatre.com/events

Sloane Square London, SW1W 8AS ⊖ Sloane Square ⇌ Victoria Station
🐦 royalcourt f theroyalcourttheatre ⊚ royalcourttheatre

SUPPORT THE COURT AND BE A PART OF OUR FUTURE.

Every penny raised goes directly towards producing bold new writing for our stages, cultivating and supporting writers in the UK and around the world, and inspiring the next generation of theatre-makers.

You can make a one-off donation by text:

Text **Support 5** to 70560 to donate £5

Text **Support 10** to 70560 to donate £10

Text **Support 20** to 70560 to donate £20

Texts cost the donation amount plus one standard message. UK networks only.

To find out more about the different ways in which you can get involved, visit our website: royalcourttheatre.com/support-us

The English Stage Company at the Royal Court Theatre is a registered charity (No. 231242)

two Palestinians go dogging

Sami Ibrahim

Characters

REEM
SAYEED
JAWAD
SALWA
SARA
TARIQ
ADAM

And SOLDIERS, VILLAGERS, JOURNALISTS,
PROTESTERS, DO-GOODERS

Time

Mid-2040s.

Place

A village called Beit al-Qadir – east of Jerusalem.

Notes

Chapter titles should mostly be screamed at the audience.

A dash (–) indicates someone actively not speaking.

A sentence without a full stop is unfinished.

If possible, handkerchiefs embroidered with the flag of
Palestine should be sold on the door as the audience enters, as
well as during the interval.

*This text went to press before the end of rehearsals and so may
differ slightly from the play as performed.*

ACT ONE

Storming Palestinian hip-hop.
House lights stay up, everyone chats.
REEM enters, clutching a piece of paper.

REEM   I'm supposed to read this out before we start.
                    It's from the guy who wrote this play.

Then she hands the paper to SAYEED. *He reads it out:*

SAYEED   *WARNING*
                    The play you are about to see is not
                    pro-Palestinian.
                    Or pro-Israeli.
                    Or anti-Israeli.
                    Or anti-Palestinian.
                    Or anything that is pro or anti anyone or
                    anything that could possibly be construed as

REEM snatches the piece of paper, throws it away.

REEM   My god, is this serious? Did he have a gun to
                    his head when he wrote this?

REEM looks at the audience.

                    I'm starting with a joke: two Palestinians,
                    couple of women, about to go dogging.
                    It's late at night, middle of nowhere, both
                    getting in the mood, and one says to the other
                    Man, you are gonna love it, there's all these
                    Arab hunks and you just get to fuck 'em.
                    and the other one's like
                    Yum.
                    and the first one goes
                    Sometimes, I wish some Israelis would turn
                    up, cos I'd sling on a strap-on and fuck them,
                    right in the arse, fuck them so hard they'll
                    know what it's like to get occupied.
                    and the other one goes

Oh snap
cos the first one's just been tied up, arrested,
slung into the back of a van, and you thought
this was a joke, but it's not, it's serious, this is
a Serious Play About Palestine.
No one is allowed to laugh.
So fuck you, go home, have some respect –
here's the prologue:
<u>Two Palestinians Go Dogging</u>

Beat.

I'm kidding – of course you can laugh.
But only if I say something funny.
And dogging is not funny.

SAYEED   It's quite funny.

REEM   Shut up Sayeed.
That's Sayeed, by the way.
Reem and Sayeed: I'm the clever one, he's
the twat.

SAYEED   Please don't call me a twat.

REEM   But I love him really. We're gonna go
dogging. Aren't we?

SAYEED   I hope so.

REEM   Of course we are, but first – we are gonna
need a lot of context.
The year is twenty forty-three.
Half of you are dead, the other half are voting
Tory, things are tense.
People are on edge, the Fifth Intifada is right
around the corner.
And we'll get to that in a minute but right
now, we're gonna have outdoor sex.
Two important things about where we are.
Number one: we are on a contested piece of
land, near to our village of Beit al-Qadir,
which is next to a settlement, which is east of
Jerusalem.
Strict security, IDF patrols.

Number two: for Palestinians, this is a
dogging hotspot.
Every Thursday.
We get turned on by the risk.
I'm serious: google it.

VILLAGERS *join them, one by one.*
They all assume the dogging position.

It starts with a bit of touching.
We're not completely naked, just pants-
round-the-ankles-sort-of-thing.
Small group of us – but people come and go.
–
That's funny, by the way, that deserves a
bigger laugh: come and go.
Whatever.
Things start heating up.
You can feel all the rough Palestinian hands.
All slipping over each other, scraping, sparks
flying, as our hands fumble and sweat – and
sometimes nails scratch, and blisters catch,
and it's all desperate. A bit too panicked, a bit
too clammy.

They all start growling – like dogs.
And as the dogging heats up, the growls will turn to barks, will
turn to full-on climactic howling.

And I know it's dark but my eyes are getting
used to it so I can make out Sayeed's outline
as someone grabs on to him. I can see a hand
connected to an arm, to a body, and I can't tell
if the body's a man or a woman but it doesn't
matter cos it's
It's nice.
So I help – I grab on to Sayeed. And someone
tries grabbing on to me.
It's very nice.
They focus on me as I focus on Sayeed.
And we all just keep going.
And going.

> And going.
> And
> And
> And
> AND

Climax.
Blackout.
Searchlights.
Panic and shouts.
Gunshots.
Silence.
Lights up.
REEM *is standing. Everyone else is crouched on the floor.*

> And sometimes we get caught. Everyone alright?

VILLAGERS *pick themselves up, brush themselves down. They start to clear out.*
SAYEED *joins* REEM.

> I mean, it's worth the risk.
> But sometimes we get caught.
> Question:
> If a Palestinian doesn't have an IDF sniper trained on them, are they even a Palestinian?
> Don't answer, it's a stupid question, we just love dogging.
> Right.
> Who wants to play a game? Anyone?
> C'mon, have some enthusiasm – chapter one:
> Bibi Says
> Which is a bit like Simon Says.
> Except with Bibi – and Bibi is the nickname for Benjamin Netanyahu.
> I don't know about you but I think 'Bibi' is a very cute nickname for a man who is quite obviously a cunt.
> I'm joking, I'm joking, it's a joke, I'm joking.
> But he is a cunt.
> Bibi says… put your hands on your head.

Beat.

SAYEED   The woman's telling you to put your hands on
                your head.

The audience does so.

REEM   There we go, that's better!
                Bibi says… start clapping.
                Bibi says stop clapping!
                Um… stamp your feet.
                Very good, you remember the rules to Bibi
                Says!
                Bibi says… be complicit in the oppression of
                the Palestinian people.
                Phwoar that's a bit much, isn't it?
                This is meant to be a fun night out.
                Bibi says build a settlement – BAM!

A settlement pops up – some SOLDIERS *build it.*

                Bibi says build another settlement – BAM!

And another pops up.

                Okay… Destroy a settlement.
                Ahhhhh, that's not what Bibi says!
                Bibi never says destroy a settlement. What
                a laugh. What else does he say?
                Bibi says make Jerusalem our eternal and
                undivided capital.

SAYEED   Bibi says move the embassy.

REEM   Bibi says it's just self-defence.

SAYEED   Bibi says this is a bit of a pro-Palestinian
                love-in.

REEM   Bibi says try to see our perspective.

SAYEED   Bibi says 'Israel will not rest until the death
                of Sara Yadin is avenged.'

REEM   Bibi says

SAYEED   who's Sara Yadin?

REEM   Which is a good question.

SAYEED   I know.

REEM	And we should answer it.
SAYEED	Absolutely.
REEM	Sara Yadin is an Israeli. And she's dead.
SAYEED	And Bibi wants to know, how did she die?
REEM	Another excellent question. Cos I'm here to tell you about the Fifth Intifada. And if I want to do that, I gotta start with the death of Sara Yadin – chapter two: <u>There's a Bloke on the Telly Talking About His Dead Daughter</u>

The telly is on – Bibi and ADAM *stand next to each other.*

SAYEED	Reem?
REEM	Yes.
SAYEED	There's a bloke on the telly talking about his dead daughter.
REEM	Is that right?
SAYEED	Oh yes.
REEM	Before we go on, have you noticed that my husband's a bit thick?
SAYEED	Excuse me?
REEM	What?
SAYEED	What did you say?
REEM	NOVEMBER TWENTY FORTY-THREE The start of the Intifada. And we're jumping ahead here, but the bloke on the telly is called Adam.
SAYEED	A bit wet, crying a lot, arm in arm with Bibi.
REEM	His dead daughter is Sara Yadin. And he stands next to Bibi, on the telly, talking about her.

SAYEED   By the way, at this point Bibi is *old*.

REEM   He got kicked out of office.

SAYEED   Remember that?

REEM   He divorced, he faced corruption charges, he
beat corruption charges, he remarried, he
became head of the UN, he got fired, he
remarried again, he even died – but they
resurrected him and his reanimated corpse
became prime minister.
He is eternal.
Bibi and Adam, Adam and Bibi
at a press conference because the body of
Sara Yadin has been found.
And Adam says he's sad that his daughter is
dead.

SAYEED   Which you would be, wouldn't you.

REEM   And Bibi nods along for a bit – very sad, very
sad

SAYEED   And then he says

REEM   He declares

SAYEED   Israel will not rest until the death of Sara
Yadin is avenged.

REEM   So what happens?

SAYEED   Israel does not rest until the death of Sara
Yadin is avenged.

REEM   Now 'avenged' is a very fluid term.

SAYEED *takes out a dictionary: he's a pedant and this is his
prop.*

SAYEED   The Oxford English Dictionary says: 'To
exact reasonable satisfaction for a
wrongdoing by punishing the wrongdoer.'

REEM   Except Bibi is not the kind of pansy who
sticks to definitions.

SAYEED   No.

REEM   No, he doesn't want *reasonable* satisfaction –
              Bibi wants to cripple a nation.
              But we are Palestine.
              We like to fight back.

SAYEED   We like to have an Intifada.

REEM   Define 'Intifada'.

SAYEED *flicks through his dictionary.*

SAYEED   The Oxford English Dictionary says: 'a
              Palestinian uprising against the Israeli
              occupation of

REEM   It's when Palestinians are pissed off at being
              endlessly oppressed so we chuck a whole load
              of rocks.

SAYEED   And sometimes we fire rockets. And plant
              bombs. And

REEM   And we've already had four of them.

SAYEED   And Bibi reckons he can handle another.

REEM   And we reckon, he doesn't stand a chance –
              chapter three:
              <u>The Mess We're Stuck In</u>

SAYEED *joins the* VILLAGERS, *who build the village of Beit
al-Qadir – they manoeuvre around Israeli settlements to do so.
There's a lot of chain-metal fences, barbed wire, concrete –*
REEM *makes her voice heard above the construction.*

              First things first:
              before the Intifada, we've gotta backtrack, cos
              Sara Yadin doesn't just die, just like that,
              she's killed.
              By three Palestinians.
              Except you should know that these
              Palestinians are kids.
              And these kids don't just kill Sara cos they
              want to do it, they do it cos there's a context.
              And maybe they're murderers, maybe they

don't deserve a context, but I reckon everyone
deserves a context.
And maybe I'm biased but I don't care, I'm
gonna give them a context.
The context is Beit al-Qadir.
Last Palestinian stronghold on the West Bank.

A 'Welcome to Beit al-Qadir' sign is put up.

AUGUST TWENTY FORTY-THREE
We're an hour east of Jerusalem.
Surrounded by Israeli settlements.
And our village is declared illegal.
Which means the Israelis want to demolish it
and replace it with a settlement.
Now, most people reckon Bibi likes to build
settlements because he's an arsehole, but he's
actually doing it because he's an arsehole.

Beat.

SAYEED   I like that joke.

REEM   Me too.
            The real explanation is this: one road runs
            north to south along the West Bank – it
            connects Northern Palestine to Southern
            Palestine.
            That road runs through our village and if our
            village is destroyed, that road is destroyed.
            If that road is destroyed, then the north is no
            longer connected to the south and the
            possibility of a joined-up Palestinian state
            goes up in flames – so it's quite important that
            our village isn't destroyed.
            Also, it's literally where we live so please
            fuck off.
            First, the army declared our village illegal.

SAYEED   Then the courts decided it wasn't illegal.

REEM   Then the army said it definitely was illegal
            and they brought in bulldozers.

SAYEED   Then the courts stopped the bulldozers.

REEM	Then the army brought in soldiers.
SAYEED	Then the courts said 'what are the soldiers doing?'
REEM	Then the army said it was top secret.
SAYEED	Then the courts said 'well, make sure they don't demolish anything.'
REEM	Then the soldiers demolished a couple of buildings.
SAYEED	Then the courts said 'we told you not to do that.'
REEM	Then the army sort of shrugged and was like 'whoops!'
SAYEED	Then the courts said 'don't do it again.'
REEM	Then the army sent in more soldiers.
SAYEED	Then the courts got distracted by another village being made illegal
REEM	At which point more soldiers got sent in and we took things into our own hands.
SAYEED	Protests.
REEM	And I lead them. Because I am a good human being who cares about her community.
SAYEED	No you're not.
REEM	I am.
SAYEED	You are…

SAYEED *flicks through his dictionary.*

	A little vain.
REEM	Can you blame me?
SAYEED	You are volatile.
REEM	I am NOT volatile.

He shuts his dictionary.

SAYEED	Your hobbies are limited to *Arab Idol* and cooking lentils and having sex in fields late at night.
REEM	Well. Be that as it may.
SAYEED	So tell them why you really do it.
REEM	Why?
SAYEED	I mean, if you want to.
REEM	Knock knock.
SAYEED	What?
REEM	I don't have time to be sentimental, Sayeed, I'm trying to keep this light: knock knock.
SAYEED	Who's there?
REEM	–
SAYEED	Who's
REEM	No one this is all a distraction while the IDF drives a tank through your back garden and machine-guns your family! – You can laugh, it's a good joke.
SAYEED	Funny.
REEM	Thank you. Now: the protests, when they start, they go well – chapter four: <u>The Mess We Make</u>

Now VILLAGERS *start to assemble. They start a hubbub, cheering louder and louder.*

> In fact, they go very well.
> So well that the soldiers back down.
> So well that the soldiers have to use rubber bullets.

VILLAGERS *duck from the rounds and rounds of shots – above the sound of popping bullets:*

>   And we fight back with chants and stones.

Soft at first, a chant rises:

VILLAGERS	Free
	Free
	Palestine

| REEM | Louder! |

VILLAGER	Free
	Free
	Palestine

| REEM | LOUDER! |

VILLAGER	FREE
	FREE
	PALEST

A car bomb goes off.
Silence.
Through the dust there's a voice.

REEM   I should say the protests go well until they
                turn to shit.
                OCTOBER TWENTY FORTY-THREE

Then the dust clears to reveal four figures: SARA *tied up,* JAWAD *behind her,* SALWA *and* TARIQ *in front.*
There's also a cinder block.

>   And they turn to shit when someone sets off
>   a car bomb.
>   In the middle of a protest – chapter five:
>   Three Kids and a Soldier are Stuck in the
>   Basement.

| SALWA | Her eyes look like they'll melt down her face. |

| REEM | Aka: The Cinder Block |

| SALWA | The rest of her body is dead against it. |

| REEM | This is Salwa. |
| | Salwa is watching the soldier who is |

SALWA	stained and bloody and stinking.
REEM	Salwa does not want to be here
SALWA	in this basement, with the smell, the sweat, the
REEM	fear in her eyes as she focuses on this soldier
SALWA	this girl who is frail, not even conscious
REEM	as Jawad grabs on to her head
SALWA	he stops her falling. And as her head sways I can see the mole on the back of her neck. She barely registers him. Then Jawad pulls her head back and she's upright. Eyes faded. And Jawad doesn't have a clue.
REEM	Jawad hasn't figured out who she is.
SALWA	Even though he's the one who kidnapped her.
JAWAD	I didn't kidnap her.
SALWA	Who kidnapped this soldier
REEM	in uniform
SALWA	who forced us to be here.
JAWAD	You didn't have to be here.
SALWA	Who's shaking now.
JAWAD	I'm not shaking. It's hot. The air's wet. It's
SALWA	dank, we're in a cramped basement, cinder blocks, stink of shit.
REEM	And Jawad holds a knife.
SALWA	At her neck.
REEM	Cos he's panicked.
SALWA	He wants to threaten her.

REEM	He wants to scare her.
SALWA	And now he's decided he wants to film her.
JAWAD	Take out your phone.
TARIQ	What?
JAWAD	Tariq – just do it.
TARIQ	Why?
JAWAD	Because we've gotta do something with her.
SALWA	She's freezing.
JAWAD	I know she is.
SALWA	Your knife's scratching at her neck.
JAWAD	That's the point, Tariq, take out your phone, start filming.
TARIQ	What, you want me to film her dying?
JAWAD	No, no one's dying, it's just meant to be
TARIQ	What?
JAWAD	Like a threat – just a threat – that's all.
TARIQ	Shit this is bad.
JAWAD	Trust me, it is fine, it sends a message.
SALWA	What message?
TARIQ	She's a soldier.
JAWAD	Exactly.
TARIQ	What do you mean *exactly*?
JAWAD	I mean it shows we're doing something.
TARIQ	You're in too deep now cousin.
JAWAD	So tell me what else to do.
TARIQ	Maybe we should leave her.
JAWAD	We can't just leave her. Salwa?

SALWA   Don't look at me.

JAWAD   Then say something.

SALWA   This is all on you.

JAWAD   She had a gun, she'd've killed us.

SALWA   But she didn't.

JAWAD   That's not the point.

SALWA   So what, you want to kill her?

TARIQ   You said no one's dying.

JAWAD   No one is, this is just

SALWA   Just what?

JAWAD   I dunno, just tell me where to make the cut.

SALWA   I'm not answering that.

JAWAD   Tariq.

TARIQ   I don't know.

SALWA   We're not here.

JAWAD   You are here, you're stuck here.

SALWA   But I'm not part of this.

JAWAD   But you haven't left have you?

TARIQ   I want to leave.

JAWAD   Tariq, I swear to god, if I'm making a cut then
             you're right there next to me, and if I'm not
             going to make a cut then you have to tell me
             to stop.

SALWA   –

TARIQ   –

JAWAD   Say something.

TARIQ   I don't know.

JAWAD   I'm gonna do it.

| SALWA | Don't do it. |

| TARIQ | SHIT. |

JAWAD *makes a cut.*
It's a small cut. But blood seeps out of the wound.
They all watch SARA.

| JAWAD | Bollocks. |

| TARIQ | – |

| SALWA | – |

| JAWAD | Tariq, you gotta film it. |

| TARIQ | Seriously? |

| JAWAD | What, you wanna get your sister to do it? |

| TARIQ | No. |

| JAWAD | Then get your phone out. |

TARIQ *takes out his phone, starts filming.*
As the following plays out, SALWA *finds a small plastic ID on the floor.*

| TARIQ | There's nothing there, you barely cut her. |

| JAWAD | Fuck off, it's proper, I cut her, I slit her neck. |

| TARIQ | Jesus Christ. |

| JAWAD | What are you doing? |

| TARIQ | It's not working. |

| JAWAD | Turn the flash on. |

TARIQ *gets in closer, turns on the flash* – JAWAD *reveals* SARA*'s neck.*

| | You got it? |

| TARIQ | Maybe. |

| JAWAD | I said have you got it? |

| TARIQ | Yes. |

JAWAD   Then post it.

TARIQ   What? I'm not posting anything.

JAWAD *lets* SARA *drop to the floor.*

JAWAD   You have to let everyone see.

TARIQ   What if they find us?

JAWAD   Stop being a coward.

JAWAD *grabs the phone.* TARIQ *tries to grab it back.*

TARIQ   Give it back.

JAWAD   Get off me.

JAWAD *keeps the phone away from* TARIQ *– they continue to fight over it.*

               How'd you post this thing?

TARIQ   Jawad.

JAWAD   How do I post it?

TARIQ   Jawad

JAWAD   Get off me man.

TARIQ   JAWAD GIVE ME MY FUCKING PHONE
               BACK.

JAWAD   Fine.

JAWAD *chucks the phone back to* TARIQ.

               It just died anyway.

TARIQ   For fuck's sake.

JAWAD   And it didn't send.

JAWAD *turns to* SALWA. SALWA *tries to hide the ID, but can't find a pocket.*

               Gimme yours.

SALWA   No.

JAWAD   Why not?

SALWA	Cos it's mine.

Pause.

JAWAD	What?
SALWA	What?
JAWAD	You picked something up.
SALWA	I didn't.
JAWAD	What have you got in your hand?
SALWA	Nothing. Just something I found.
JAWAD	Where?
SALWA	On the floor.
JAWAD	Show me then.
SALWA	No.
JAWAD	Don't be a dick.
SALWA	It's mine, I found it.
JAWAD	What did you find?

Now SARA *starts moaning.*

SALWA	Jawad, she's in pain.
JAWAD	She's fine, she's barely conscious.
SALWA	So maybe you should help her.
JAWAD	*You* can help her after you show me what's in your hand.

JAWAD *tries to snatch the ID – but* SALWA *slaps him away.*

I'll give it back, I just want to see.

SALWA *still doesn't move.*

Tariq, cover her mouth.

TARIQ *does so and* SARA *starts to struggle.*

Give it to me or I'll make her scream properly.

SALWA *hands the ID over.*

SALWA   Arsehole.

JAWAD *looks at it. He recognises the name. He looks at her.*

REEM   She's called Sara Yadin.
               Which means what happens next is not an
               accident.
               But also, it's not *not* an accident.

SARA *bites* TARIQ*'s hand.*

TARIQ   SHITTING HELL.

JAWAD *chucks the ID on the floor, moves over to* SARA.

SARA   Stay back. Stay back.

JAWAD   You speak Arabic?

SARA   A little.

JAWAD   Fuck.

SARA   Let me go and nothing will happen.

JAWAD   FUCK.

SALWA   Just let her go.

JAWAD   We can't.

SALWA   Why?

JAWAD   Cos then we're dead aren't we?

SARA   I promise you won't be.

JAWAD   I'm meant to believe that?

SARA   Please.

Now SARA *is moving closer to* JAWAD.

JAWAD   What are you doing?

SARA   I am begging you.

JAWAD   Get away from me, I've got a knife.

But SARA *lunges at* JAWAD *and* JAWAD *shoves her away.*
Quiet.
And then:

SARA   HELP.
              HELP.
              HELP.

SARA *screams and keeps screaming.*

TARIQ   What do we do?

JAWAD   She needs to stop screaming, people will hear.

TARIQ   So shut her up.

JAWAD *kicks* SARA.

SALWA   You don't need to kick her.

JAWAD   She won't stop.

SALWA   Stop kicking then.

TARIQ   Shut her up

JAWAD   Stop screaming, STOP.

Spotlight on SALWA.

SALWA   Very suddenly Jawad has a cinder block in his
              hands and it's balanced over Sara Yadin's head.
              It's half a joke and half not a joke and Tariq's
              fled the room already.
              The cinder block shuts Sara Yadin up.
              Because it would. A cinder block. Eight
              centimetres above you.
              Seven centimetres. Nine centimetres. Sara
              Yadin's eyes watch it.
              And then she watches me.
              And with those eyes she begs me

SARA   Can you hear me?

SALWA   She tells me

SARA   I was put on guard duty.
              I was a glorified CCTV camera guarding a
              settlement and it was pissing with rain.
              I hated it.
              Seventy-six days before I cut up my ID card
              and I'm meant to be done.

	Out. I'm not meant to be here.
SALWA	But Jawad can't hear and Jawad is trembling now and the block is slipping onto
SARA	I'm meant to be off my head in a club in Tel Aviv.
SALWA	It is slipping from the hands of the fighter onto the head of the soldier.
SARA	I'm meant to be home. I just came in here for shelter. Caught in the blast. Brain oozing. Turned around and he was there, hiding.
SALWA	This fighter who's a fighter because she's a soldier, this soldier who's a soldier because he's a fighter.
SARA	What are you doing?
SALWA	I step back. And before I leave I look at Jawad. He looks at me and
SARA	What are you doing?
SALWA	I'm nodding at Jawad. Just a small nod. I think. Or a shake of the head. I think. And I look down at Sara Yadin. And as my eyes drop humidity rains onto the floor. And as my eyes drop the cinder block drops. Dead weight. And I've left the room before the crunch of concrete on bone.

Lights up.
SARA *is squashed under a cinder block. There's a lot of blood.*
REEM *watches it for a while –* SAYEED*'s there too and*
JAWAD*'s in the background.*

REEM   Bloody hell.
                     Um.
                     We should probably... could we

Some SOLDIERS *come on.*

                     Yeah, we should clean that up.

The SOLDIERS *take away her body.* JAWAD *watches on, not
quite sure what to do.*

                     Thanks.

Breath.

SAYEED   You alright?

REEM   I'm fine.
                     Jawad is arrested soon after – after he's
                     abandoned by the others.

SAYEED   *Abandoned* – is that true?

REEM   It is true Sayeed because that's how I'm
                     telling it and it's how Jawad tells it – chapter
                     six:
                     <u>How Jawad Tells It</u>
                     Poor boy is covered in blood.
                     Aren't you?

JAWAD *nods.*

                     Go on then.

*He gets out a tube of fake blood and starts covering himself
in it.*

                     Covered in blood – Sara's blood, I should
                     specify.
                     Mingled with sweat and dust.
                     The only sound is his soft, slow breathing.

JAWAD *stands up straight. He breathes. The blood has formed
a puddle around his feet.*

And I don't want you to think we're ignoring
the dead Sara Yadin, because we're not, we
will get to her.
But, for now, this is Jawad's story.
So tell us.

JAWAD   Now?

REEM   Right now.

               –

JAWAD   Okay. There is this halo of blood on the floor.

REEM   It coagulates in his boot print.

JAWAD   And if my breath speeds out of control I get
               scared, I get nervous, but

JAWAD's *alone*.

               if I'm steady I feel like Rambo.

*He pretends he's got a machine gun in his hands. He fires it into
the audience.*

               du du du du du du du du du du du du du du du
               du du du du du du du du du du du du du du du
               du du

               –

               du

Then he drops his fake machine gun.

               Makes my head woozy.

               –

               Very slowly and without explanation, the
               ceiling is falling in.
               Not collapsing.
               Just slowly descending.
               So that it crushes my forehead.
               I try standing completely still, try using my
               forehead to keep the bricks from crushing me.
               Breathe. Control my heart.

               –

               On the floor is the ID card of Sara Yadin.
               There is a sense, in my mind, that I should
               pick it up, and take it, and maybe destroy it.

But the ceiling is applying so much pressure
to my head that I cannot bring my eyes to
focus.
And I remain standing, softly breathing, over
the body of Sara Yadin for roughly ten hours.
My body doesn't need food or water.
Just stillness: it takes the full ten hours to
bring my heart rate back to normal.
And once that's done and once night is
finished and it's morning, I leave.
I am now hungry and I will purchase some
mana'eesh from a local bakery.
I will eat this mana'eesh sitting in the cold
morning sun.
I will get strange looks.
Then I will remember that I am covered in
blood.
I will think, it can't be that much blood.
So I'll ask a stranger for a napkin to wipe it off.
The stranger will turn out to be a soldier.
I will smile at the soldier and try speaking to
him in Hebrew.

Upbeat, he speaks to the SOLDIER (*possibly with a thick accent*).

A big fuck off to you my twat-faced brother.

Then he realises what he's said.

I will forget that the only Hebrew words
I know are swear words.
I will be arrested.

JAWAD *starts wiping the blood off with a napkin.*
REEM *bursts back on –* SAYEED *follows.*

REEM   And that's what they do, they arrest him.

SAYEED   I know.

REEM   Just because he's a Palestinian wandering the
                streets covered in blood – not even his blood
                – they think they have a right to arrest him!

FASCISTS.
Can you actually believe it?!

SAYEED   Yes I can.

REEM   Shut up Sayeed.
                They arrest him.
                And the poor boy doesn't know what to do.
                One minute he's asking for a napkin, the next
                there are
                Thirty soldiers
                Forty soldiers
                Fifty soldiers

JAWAD   It is three soldiers.

REEM   A hundred soldiers surrounding one boy.
                Fear taking over, and regret, and not
                understanding the situation he's trapped in.
                All of that, all at once.
                Panic floods his brain and he can't move.

When he's basically clean, JAWAD *rolls his eyes and leaves.*

                But his body is calm.
                Stoic.
                He is a human being.
                Delicate.
                Scared.
                Caught in a cycle of violence.
                Hounded down by the authorities.
                Trapped.
                A single Palestinian.
                Surrounded by Israelis.
                Guns trained at his head.
                Lucky to be alive.
                Fear in the face of arrest.
                And his only crime…
                His ethnicity.
                –

SAYEED   Reem, he dropped a block of concrete on
                someone's head.

REEM	Yeah. Well. You know.
SAYEED	What do I know?
REEM	He was scared.

SAYEED *is looking through his dictionary.*

SAYEED	Scared is defined as: 'the act of being fearful or frightened'. Which is not what happens when someone drops a concrete block onto a human head.
REEM	It could've slipped.
SAYEED	Slip: 'to accidentally slide or move out of position'.
REEM	Oh stop it Sayeed.
SAYEED	So it accidentally slid or moved out of position from the floor and onto a human head?
REEM	Maybe.
SAYEED	'A mere possibility or probability.'
REEM	I'm not enjoying this.
SAYEED	Neither am I.
REEM	Arsehole.
SAYEED	Look, I get you wanna protect him but he doesn't deserve
REEM	A decent defence?
SAYEED	To be let off the hook.
REEM	So you want to blame him?
SAYEED	I don't know who else to blame.
REEM	He's your son and you want to blame him?
SAYEED	Yes. Because he can handle the responsibility.
REEM	I see.
SAYEED	Reem.

REEM	–
SAYEED	Reem, come on.
REEM	He's our son by the way, I can't remember if we said that. That's why the story matters cos he's our son. I mean it matters cos it's Palestine and everything matters, but also he's our son so that matters too. Tariq and Salwa are Sayeed's brother's kids. Except Sayeed's brother's dead so the cousins spend their time hanging around our place. It's a small village.
SAYEED	You know what? I think we need a break.
REEM	No we don't.
SAYEED	Yes we do Reem.
REEM	Jawad's arrested but he reveals nothing. So it takes a week for Sara Yadin to be found. Sara Yadin is simply reported missing and a manhunt begins. And before a body is even found she becomes a symbol. And when she is found she becomes even more of a symbol, a symbol of Everything. Sara was a soldier. She was a settler. She was hard-working. She was lazy. She was young. She was beautiful. She loved her father. She loved Israel. She hated Palestine. She hated Israel. She loved Palestine. She hated Palestinian hummus. She hated Israeli hummus.

She looked good with a gun.
She never touched a gun.
She wanted peace.
She could kill an Arab at five hundred yards.
She was a party animal.
She was a loner.
She was an innocent, an icon, Joan of Arc,
the muscular, reincarnated spirit of David
Ben-Gurion.
She was scared.
Brave.
Stupid.
Sexy.
She was all things to all people and Israel will
not rest until the death of Sara Yadin is
avenged.
Until Israel triumphs.
And Palestine suffers.
And Israel Palestine Israel Palestine
It's all bollocks and it all goes on and on and
you know what?
We should have a break.

SAYEED   Thank you.

REEM   Just a moment.
              To breathe – chapter seven:
              The Story About Palestine in Which Israel is
              Not Mentioned

VILLAGERS *enter.*
Tea is poured.
They add sugar to the tea, they stir the tea.
REEM *and* SAYEED *join them and pour themselves some tea.*
*Tea poured, they all look at each other, nod, and take a seat: it's
like the chapter's about to begin.*
And then nothing is said for a long time.
Someone coughs.
Another pause.

SAYEED   So…

REEM   Nothing about Israel remember!

Another pause.

VILLAGER 1   Did... anyone... see the... football...?

VILLAGER 2   Yes.

VILLAGER 1   Good football?

VILLAGER 2   Good football.

VILLAGERS   GOOD FOOTBALL.

A really long pause.

REEM   This is rubbish.
　　　　　The amount of time spent on this isn't worth
　　　　　the joke.
　　　　　C'mon, clear off, get out.

VILLAGERS *leave. Apart from one – the actor who plays*
ADAM.

　　　　　What are you doing?

ADAM *doesn't move.*

　　　　　Question: if a story about Palestine doesn't
　　　　　feature a tortured examination of the Arab-
　　　　　Israeli conflict, is it even a story about
　　　　　Palestine?

ADAM *picks up a paintbrush and a tin of paint.*

　　　　　Except you don't need to respond cos here
　　　　　comes someone to remind us that the answer
　　　　　is always a firm fucking NO.

ADAM *paints a portion of the stage a bright red – and then*
leaves.

　　　　　That's the Red Zone.

From now on, no Palestinian character enters the Red Zone
unless explicitly stated.

　　　　　In case you're wondering.
　　　　　So you can guess what this chapter's gonna
　　　　　be called – chapter eight:
　　　　　The Red Zone

>   The Israelis mark it out as soon as news of
>   Sara's disappearance gets out.
>   It's a 'neutral area' between Beit al-Qadir and
>   the settlement next door.
>   Supposed to quell tensions.
>   Except it's not really neutral cos settlers are
>   allowed to enter it and we're not.
>   Allow me to demonstrate.

REEM *and* VILLAGERS *stand next to the Red Zone.*
REEM *places a toe in the Red Zone. She ducks as a bullet zips
over her head.*

>   Fucking hell. Yeah. Exactly.

Without moving, another bullet zips past.

>   ARSEHOLES. DON'T SHOOT ME
>   BEFORE I'M DONE.

Pause.

>   Thank you – chapter nine:
>   Jawad Becomes a Hero

Now VILLAGERS *all take out phones – they take photos and
videos of* JAWAD, *who stands in one corner.*

>   Jawad getting arrested is a big deal by the way.
>   It causes a storm in our village: two hundred
>   soldiers surrounding him.
>   Maybe three hundred, maybe more.

JAWAD   Just three.

REEM   Impossible to count.
             And even if you could count, it feels like
             hundreds.
             It feels electric.
             And everyone wants in on the action.
             Habibi, where's the blood gone?

JAWAD   I wiped it off.

REEM   It looks better with the blood.

JAWAD *puts a bit of blood back on his face.*
VILLAGERS *get excited and take more photos.*

> See?
> And the blood is really what does it.
> As soldiers contract around Jawad like a
> clogged artery, the Palestinians are there.
> Standing nearby, standing on houses, on
> walls, phones all held up, all recording.
> And we don't stop recording.

JAWAD   Even when I'm dragged into the back of a van.

REEM   Especially when he's dragged into the back of
               a van.

JAWAD   It makes for good telly, it goes viral.

REEM   And it means the soldiers won't shoot. Cos no
               soldier wants to be filmed shooting a
               Palestinian.

JAWAD   I mean they still arrest me.

REEM   No soldier wants to get caught by a do-gooder.

JAWAD   But it's less nasty.

REEM   Cos the do-gooders are the worst. They have
               so many opinions.

JAWAD   And my head's still thrown to the ground.
               Crushed against the gravel.

REEM   Like a fresh egg.
               We watch it happen.

JAWAD   And I'm lifted up.

REEM   And it's on TikTok, people watch it round the
               world.

JAWAD   Slipping and rocking

REEM   Although the audio's a bit fuzzy.

JAWAD   As they contort my body.

REEM	But it's worth a watch – Jawad's hands being tied up.
JAWAD	Thrown into the back of the vehicle.
REEM	Doors slammed.
JAWAD	Stuffed in.

VILLAGERS *stop taking photos, slowly exit – except for one who keeps filming from a distance.*

REEM	And the wheels spin in the mud. Most people stop caring at this point, but me and Sayeed keep watching. One person films the whole thing, puts it on YouTube, even as the vehicle takes five minutes to get out of the mud. And when the jeep escapes we watch it disappear. And then we wait. Me and Sayeed. At our computer. We wait. And then the Wi-Fi cuts.

Now all go apart from REEM *and* SAYEED.

SAYEED	One neighbour tells us Jawad's fine.
REEM	Another neighbour says he's dead.
SAYEED	That neighbour's an arsehole though.
REEM	And a liar.
SAYEED	Who owes me money.
REEM	Then another neighbour says turn on the telly.
SAYEED	Which we do.
REEM	And we see Jawad's face on the telly. Actual telly, not YouTube, not Facebook, not even Arab telly, actual BBC telly. The do-gooders have found the footage. The do-gooders do good.

International pressure.
The plight of Palestine, et cetera, et cetera,
wonderful stuff!
You gotta give it to the do-gooders, if they
wanna do good, they do good.
Let's hear it for the do-gooders!

SAYEED   The do-gooders who completely ignore the
fact that Jawad has killed someone.

REEM   Oh shut up Sayeed.
Let's hear it for the do-gooders!

REEM *starts clapping.*

Woooooooooo!
C'mon, clap with me!

REEM *quickly stops clapping.*

Jawad still goes on trial.

SAYEED   And obviously he's found guilty.

REEM   But it's not a fair trial.

SAYEED   Except the kid is guilty. So he's found guilty.
Because he's guilty.

He flicks through his dictionary.

'Culpable or responsible for a specific
wrongdoing.'

REEM   Yes, well done.

SAYEED   In this case a very specific wrongdoing and
the system fucks him for it.
And his cousins run and they get fucked too
cos no one gets away.
It's a fact of life, we all have to learn it.

REEM   –

SAYEED   You're looking at me like I've said something
remarkable, but open your eyes Reem, it's
obvious.

He finds the right page in his dictionary.

	It is 'easily-perceived or understood. Self-evident'.
REEM	Put that thing away.
SAYEED	Tell them about Tariq then.
REEM	Put it away.
SAYEED	I'll put it away if you tell them about Tariq.

They stare at each other – slowly, SAYEED *lowers his dictionary.*
TARIQ *appears.*

REEM	Chapter ten: <u>Tariq Gets Fucked</u> Cousin number one. Who tries
TARIQ	to escape over the roof of a settlement building and gets caught in barbed wire. They line the walls with it. And I think I can make it over. But then I feel a snag. And at first I think Oh it's just my jeans so I keep going, try to rip at my jeans but then I realise that adrenalin does a good job of hiding pain. And it's my skin that's caught, not the denim. And as I move that pain can't be hidden for long. I let out this very long and very angry scream.

TARIQ *is caught, on barbed wire, on the roof of a settlement.*

REEM	And can you guess who hears the scream?
SAYEED	Who?
REEM	Everyone! And can you guess what they do about it?
SAYEED	I don't know.

REEM	Nothing!
TARIQ	Nothing?
REEM	People see him, and by people I mean settlers. They see him and they don't help him. They don't call the army in either, they just They sort of nod at him. Or they give him a sad smile. Or they tilt their head at him like they're saying *Sorry pal that must be pretty crap for you up there!* And then they walk on and leave him. – He's an actual kid and people just leave him.
SAYEED	Reem?
REEM	What?
SAYEED	You wanna hear a secret?
REEM	Not particularly.
SAYEED	I would do the same.
TARIQ	Seriously? Ammo?
REEM	You don't mean that.
SAYEED	I do.
REEM	No you don't.
SAYEED	If he wasn't my nephew I wouldn't know what to do and I would probably end up leaving him and I reckon you would too.
REEM	You shouldn't speak like that.
SAYEED	Like what?
REEM	Like you're not on our side.
SAYEED	I just think you need to climb down off that high horse.
REEM	And I think you need to stop talking like a

SAYEED   –

REEM   –

SAYEED   A what?

REEM   Nothing.

SAYEED   You were going to call me a

              –

REEM   But I didn't.

SAYEED   But you almost called me a

REEM *looks around.*

REEM   So what word do you want me to use Sayeed?

SAYEED   –

REEM   Go on, tell me, look it up in your stupid
              dictionary.

SAYEED *doesn't look it up.*

              Why's it so quiet?
              It's what the Arabic translates as.
              We call them *Jews*.
              And they call us *Arabs*, by the way.
              They don't differentiate, we don't
              differentiate, so that's what we're left with:
              Arabs and Jews, us and them, and right now
              he's speaking like he's on their side.
              You English. You're here for some
              authenticity, you want the truth, but you get
              all funny when you hear it, so maybe it's
              better if we just say Israelis and Palestinians.
              Agreed?

SAYEED   –

REEM   What is it?

SAYEED   You need to tell them that it is wrong to hold
              Jews collectively responsible for the actions
              of the state of Israel.

REEM	Well obviously.
SAYEED	Good.
REEM	Good.
	–
SAYEED	So tell them about cousin number two.
REEM	Salwa.
SAYEED	Who also gets fucked.
REEM	Except the story of how Salwa gets fucked is a long one.
	So long it's going to take three whole chapters to tell – strap yourself in.
	It all begins with Sara Yadin.
SAYEED	Sara Yadin who's dead.
REEM	Who is dead. And is a... Not a...
SAYEED	Yes, well done, Reem.

REEM *is pleased with herself for saying the right thing.*
Meanwhile, SARA *appears onstage.*

REEM	Chapter eleven.
	<u>Sara Wakes Up.</u>
SARA	It's dawn
	or dusk.
REEM	That is Sara's spirit speaking.
SARA	It's hard to tell from the half-light stretching across the room.
REEM	And I don't know how her spirit can speak given it doesn't have vocal cords but whatever.
	The spirit of Sara Yadin detaches from her body a few days after her death.
	Because her body is unburied, her spirit cannot pass to the next life.
	So her spirit just sits there.

	Uncertain. Hanging about. Waiting. Her head
SARA	is buzzing, it's
REEM	furious, takes her hours to calm down, and she has
SARA	no idea where I am or where I was and
REEM	there's someone lying in front of her – she doesn't know who but she wears
SARA	wears the same uniform
REEM	I'll take it from here thank you Sara. She wears the same uniform with
SARA	the same trousers, already
REEM	Faded and scuffed
SARA	at the knees
REEM	She's got
SARA	I've got a pair just like it
REEM	Excuse me, I'm trying to narrate this bit.

Pause.

SARA	She's got thick boots on.
REEM	God almighty.
SAYEED	Why don't you let her speak?
REEM	Cos I'm doing the talking.
SAYEED	Let her finish.
REEM	Halas. Fine. Have it your way.

Begrudgingly, REEM *steps back.*

SARA	She's got thick boots on. And I swear they're just like mine. Or maybe not cos hers are filthy.

And I'm thinking it's uncanny that this person
in front of me's dressed so similar.
And I'm also thinking an olive-green uniform
isn't so unique.
Just a little accident.
Weird that we'd meet
In this, uh
It's a dank room, one window, a basement in a
Maybe an apartment block or a
And I don't know how I've, we've ended up in
So I ask her: what are we doing?
She doesn't respond.
She's asleep. I think.
So I retrace, go back over and I
I forget.
Soil through fingers.
Cos there were
Protests and a knife and a
Cinder block.
And I see a cinder block across the room.
And she's face-down, knocked out, black hair,
all a mess, and on the back of her neck is a
mole.
Deep brown.
I reach for the back of my neck – scratch at
my mole – but it feels different, it's not
coarse, it's barely there, it's just
Not even atoms.
I see this girl's neck is, is cracked and twisted,
so she's facing up and down all at once, she's
a computer glitch.
But I'm staying calm.
Examine her face.
Strands of wet hair.
For the longest time I stare into the strangest
mirror.
And I realise that if she's still here and I'm
still there then my spirit can only ever…

REEM   Chapter twelve:
              Salwa Returns

SALWA *is in the basement.*

>Days later.
>She's been hiding, sleeping on sofas, running,
>but now

SARA   she pauses as she enters.

SALWA *stays still.*

REEM   At this point Jawad's been arrested.
                  The blood on his skin has been identified as
                  Sara Yadin's but the body is still missing.
                  Jawad refuses to speak.
                  Soldiers are on the hunt.
                  And Salwa

SARA   can't keep away.

Pause.

SALWA   So I
                  God, I don't know.

SARA   –

SALWA   I mean, you can't hear me
                  Obviously
                  You're just
                  You're there
                  But, um, I came to

SARA *walks over to* SALWA. *She stands nose to nose with*
SALWA – *but* SALWA *doesn't notice.*
Then SALWA *sees something – she stoops to pick up* SARA*'s
ID.*
SARA *watches.*

>I can make sure this is

SARA   –

SALWA   Maybe I can return it.
                  To your father or
                  I don't know.

SALWA *puts the ID in her pocket.*

>I'm so sorry.

SARA   –

SALWA   I hope your spirit has found peace.

SARA *slaps* SALWA. SALWA *doesn't react.*

REEM   And that's the moment when

Sirens – in the distance.

SALWA   Shit.

REEM   The exact moment, the sound of soldiers
                  arriving.
                  Approaching a building where they hope they
                  will find the body of Sara Yadin.
                  –
                  Run.

SALWA   –

REEM   Salwa. Run.

SALWA *runs.*
And keeps running…

                  I feel bad.
                  Because she runs but, between you and me,
                  we all know it's pointless.

…until she's exhausted.
And she stops.
And tries to catch her breath.
And then looks up.
And is about to keep going but can't.
Because SALWA *is caught in the glare of a spotlight.*
The disembodied voice of a SOLDIER *rings out:*

SOLDIER   On the ground, get on the ground.

SALWA *kneels.*

                  Raise your hands.

SALWA *raises her hands.*

                  Why were you in that building?

SALWA   I don't know.

SOLDIER	What were you doing in there?
SALWA	Nothing. Please.
SOLDIER	Are you carrying anything?
SALWA	No.
SOLDIER	Keep your hands where I can see them.
SALWA	I am not armed.
SOLDIER	Stay calm.
SALWA	I am.
	–
SOLDIER	Sara Yadin was killed in that building. Did you know that?
SALWA	–
SOLDIER	I want your name.
SALWA	Don't shoot.
SOLDIER	Then tell me your name.
SALWA	I've forgotten. I can't remember. I'm
	–
	I have the ID of Sara Yadin, that's what I was doing.
	–
	Will you give it to her father?

SALWA *is about to fumble in her pocket but is stopped:*

SOLDIER	Keep your hands raised.
SALWA	My name is Salwa Hajri. I have the ID of Sara Yadin. I am going to reach into my pocket. I am going to retrieve it and I will give it back to you and I will leave. Is that okay?

Pause. There's no answer.

I will do it slowly.

Slowly, SALWA *reaches into her pocket.*

                  I can't remember which pocket it's in.

SOLDIER   Don't mess us around.

SALWA*'s hands are shaking.*

SALWA   I'm sorry, I'm just trying to

Then, quickly, SALWA *reaches into her other pocket.*

SOLDIER   She's armed.

SALWA   I'm not armed.

SOLDIER   Then stop moving.

SALWA   I'm just

But, as SALWA *pulls the ID out, she drops it.*
And SALWA *reaches down to pick up the ID but before she can she is shot.*
The spotlight fades.
SALWA *is dead.*
SARA *stands opposite her.*

SARA   It's quieter than you think.
                  You see a body flop to the floor.
                  Then silence.
                  Then a moment later comes the sound of
                  a gunshot.
                  It's so disconnected it barely registers.

REEM   And the sound of a shot draws the
                  Palestinians out.
                  We arrive.
                  Crying and furious and fuming and stoic.
                  It is devastating.
                  Because this has happened in cold blood –
                  because this is inexcusable.
                  Like everything else.
                  And the soldiers, they have already
                  disappeared.

VILLAGERS *emerge – they lift up* SALWA *in a funeral march.*

We lift Salwa up.
She is beautiful.
She is a floating red streak – this hovercraft
on a stream of black fabrics and Palestinian
hands.
We take her to be buried.
We put the anger to one side because all that
matters is finding space for Salwa to rest.
Because if you cram a whole life into
eighteen years then you need a long rest.
You need peace.
And as we find her that peace

SARA   She slips.

REEM   We can feel her slipping.

SARA   Out of life.

REEM   She falls.

This chapter title doesn't need to be shouted.

And then – chapter thirteen:
The Fight Begins

SARA *floats above* SALWA.

SARA   Her face is so soft. And she is

SALWA   oozing, like my brain is thick gloop.
              Glaring white light in my eyes.

SALWA *is lowered. There is a loud hum.*

My body is disintegrating, it is about to melt
and seep into the earth and

SARA   her spirit starts to detach.
              As the earth is dug up.
              It detaches.

The earth is dug up – perhaps a prayer is said.
SALWA *is laid in the earth –* SARA *descends.*

As she is buried, as she is laid to rest, her
spirit disconnects.

And it will soar up to the heavens because it
is at peace.
They have found her peace.
Which is more than they found for me.

SALWA   This hum's getting louder.

SARA   Because I

SALWA   It is surging.

SARA   I have nowhere.

SALWA   Higher. Frantic.

SARA   I am stuck and she is

SALWA   Thousands of clammy hands spreading over
            me.

SARA   I need her body.

SALWA   Without the energy to stop them.

SARA   Need to pulse through her.

SALWA   Flash my eyes open.

SARA   Summon the energy.

SALWA   See

SARA   Feel me

SALWA   I see

SARA   Feel me

SALWA   Sara Yadin

SARA   Feel

SALWA   Sara Yadin

The VILLAGERS *disperse.*

SARA   Drifting

SALWA   down

SARA   to

SALWA   my

SARA	stomach
SALWA	and I whisper
SARA	and push
SALWA	NO
SARA	deeper
SALWA	her spirit
SARA	into
SALWA	my spirit
SARA	collapsing
SALWA	shuddering
SARA	and I
SALWA	she
SARA	and I step inside
SALWA	brace myself
SARA	force myself, into, *through* Salwa
SALWA	fighting
SARA	overpowering
SALWA	shrieking
SARA	curse
SALWA	attack
SARA	am brutish
SALWA	am open
SARA	am desperate
SALWA	am vulnerable
SARA	am vulnerable
SALWA	am desperate

SARA   I bear down

SALWA   I am terrified

SARA/SALWA   And we fight.

SALWA   Because Sara needs a body.

SARA   And Salwa needs a body.

SARA/SALWA   But the body is about to pass.
                 We know it.
                 We are.
                 Crashing with energy.
                 We are.
                 Exploding.
                 The body contorts.
                 Our body.
                 We fight for it.
                 It vibrates.
                 It is boiling
                 It is

SALWA   gasping

SARA   gasping

SARA/SALWA   Time slips
                 Our body is
                 Fading and fading and
                 and

SARA   Salwa

SALWA   Sara

SARA   fights

SALWA   fights

SARA   fights

SARA/SALWA   and then
                 the body
                 the spirit
                 finally
                 ascends

SARA *and* SALWA *watch the spirit ascending.*
Pause.
SARA *and* SALWA *look at each other. And then disappear.*
REEM *and* SAYEED *arrive – slowly,* REEM *picks up the*
discarded ID card, examines it, then pockets it.
There's a smile on her face.

REEM	Salwa wins, by the way. Salwa crushes Sara and she wins – chapter fourteen: <u>FUCKING WINNING</u>
SAYEED	Even though Salwa shouldn't have died in the first place.

Pause.

REEM	No.
SAYEED	So it is the smallest of victories.
REEM	But it is a victory. And it is the start of something.
SAYEED	–
REEM	Don't shrug Sayeed, because this is important. Yes, this is sad, but we aren't pathetic, we do not cry, we keep fighting. Because the Israelis declare war on us. They want vengeance for Sara Yadin. And once Salwa is killed, we want vengeance for Salwa Hajri. The two sides declare war on each other. All at once. And the story of Salwa and Sara is told at every meeting the resistance has. It is told with pride. And it is an inspiration – because Salwa is a martyr and her story lives on. The Palestinians who bury her claim they see a spirit try to steal the body of Salwa. The wandering spirit of Sara Yadin is witnessed trying to enter Salwa's body and you know what happens?

The spirit of Sara Yadin is told to fuck off.
And we tell that story.
We, Palestinians, we tell that story because it
matters, and it means something, and Salwa
may be dead but her spirit burns.
Her spirit soars in the afterlife.
When Israel attacks and Palestine fights back,
Salwa's spirit is there.
I promise you that.
After all the dead bodies, after all the
pointless deaths, Salwa's spirit soars.

SAYEED   She's still dead.

REEM   I know.

SAYEED   So how is this a win?

REEM   Because Salwa means something, because
            Salwa helps spark an Intifada.
            She is important.

SAYEED   She's dead.

REEM   And that's just semantics.

SAYEED   Excuse me?

REEM   No, obviously it's not semantics, it's just, it's

SAYEED   What?

REEM   Salwa is an inspiration.

SAYEED   She's dead.

REEM   But she spurs us on, she is an icon.

SAYEED   She's dead.

REEM   Oh give it a rest Sayeed.
            People die.
            And some people die more important deaths
            than others.
            That's life.
            That's a fact.

Pause.

SAYEED   And was Loubna's death one of the important
           ones? For example.

REEM   I don't know why you're bringing that up.

SAYEED   But was it?

REEM   Now's not the time.

SAYEED *shrugs, turns to the audience.*

SAYEED   Our daughter was killed.
           Two years ago.
           Her name was Loubna Hajri.
           She was twelve years old.
           Just so you're aware.
           An Israeli soldier came to our house, drove
           a tank up to the garden wall, hopped over,
           and fired.
           Reem does not talk about it.

REEM   –

SAYEED   And not only does she refuse to talk about it,
           but she refuses to tell you about it, and she
           refuses to engage with it, or even think about it.

REEM   That's not true.

SAYEED   Well you can say whatever you like and
           people can interpret it how they want.
           –

REEM   I do not think her death was unimportant.

SAYEED   Either way it was a death.
           On top of Salwa.
           On top of all the others.

REEM   I know.

SAYEED   But it's fine they're dead, because at least
           Reem thinks it makes for a good story!

REEM   Do you believe that?

SAYEED   I don't know. Is that what you believe?

Pause. ADAM *is present. He looks at* REEM, *she looks at him.*
Maybe he's about to speak but then:

REEM   I believe we have an Intifada to win.
              I believe those deaths – all of them – will
              matter if they help us win.
              Because I believe – right now – things are
              shit.
              Sayeed.
              Salwa has been buried.
              Jawad has been arrested.
              Tariq has been trapped and Sara Yadin has
              been found.
              Bibi is on the telly.
              Bibi stands next to Adam on the telly and
              what happens?

SAYEED   –

REEM   The army and the politicians and everyone
              else all play one big game of Bibi Says.
              What does he say?

SAYEED   Bibi says

REEM   Israel will not rest until the death of Sara
              Yadin is avenged.
              That is what Bibi says and that is what
              happens.
              And believe me, we will not rest either.
              NOVEMBER TWENTY FORTY-THREE
              The Fifth Intifada begins.
              It is terrifying.
              But I promise you this: we are going to win.
              –
              Aren't we?

SAYEED   Yes we are.

The Fifth Intifada begins.
It's gruesome and it's violent.
There are protests, there are attacks and counterattacks.
Then there is a
Blackout.

54

ACT TWO

REEM *is onstage.* SAYEED *sits in the corner reading his dictionary.*

REEM   Before we begin, I'm doing a quick survey: if you speak Arabic raise your hand…

REEM *raises her own hand (as does* SAYEED*) and waits for a few people in the audience to raise their hands. Regardless of how many people put up their hands, she keeps going:*

                Is that it? Someone in marketing needs to be fired.
                The English colonised us, gave away our country, then told us to go fuck ourselves.
                I am so tired of speaking English.

And now she starts speaking in <u>Arabic</u> *– if there are no Arabic-speakers then* REEM *can address this to* SAYEED*:*

                I'm speaking Arabic because it's so much nicer speaking Arabic isn't it?
                Now there's only us, how about we play a game?
                In order to make the English-speakers unwelcome, let's all start laughing when I say the word 'watermelon'.
                Does that make sense? Okay? Ready? Watermelon.

REEM *waits until some laughter builds –* SAYEED *laughing the loudest.*

                Come on, laugh more. Watermelon. Keep going. And one last time, make it a big one! Watermelon!

While they're laughing, REEM *switches back to* <u>English</u>*:*

I'm serious, every English person I meet, they
all do the same thing, and it is *so* annoying!
By the way, you English-speakers didn't miss
anything.
And even if you did: relax!
We've all got to learn English so you can
understand us, but do you bother learning
a syllable of Arabic?
Do you bollocks.
Sayeed, what's the word I'm looking for?

SAYEED   Ingrate.

REEM   Ingrates!

SAYEED   'A person who displays no appreciation or
kindness in return for all our goddamn hard
work, how dare you take us for granted, you
try performing in another language you twats.'

REEM   And that's exactly what the Oxford English
Dictionary says?

SAYEED   Word for word.

REEM   Fascinating.
Right, I need to stop berating people because
we're not done. Except from now on:
We only ever speak Arabic.

SAYEED   Which of course is translated into Arabic as

REEM   We only ever speak Arabic.

The dogging party assembles.
It's semi-dark.
VILLAGERS *and* REEM *and* SAYEED *all together.*

It's a Thursday and even an Intifada won't
stop us.
We've got tensions to ease.
The numbers are smaller, but we keep coming
– chapter fifteen:
Two Palestinians and an Israeli Go Dogging
Because we can't help ourselves.

The growling slowly begins.

> And it's just as it always is.
> Rough Palestinian hands.
> Lust and pumping.
> clammy and sweaty
> fingers and blisters and nails
> always
> clutching
> always
> feeling.

Then someone enters – the audience can't see who it is, but this is ADAM.
ADAM *joins in, and as he does, the growling gets louder, it turns to howling.*

> And this time we are rough.
> Violent.
> Destressing.
> Lusting.
> We are

Now the group is writhing – slowly edging closer to the Red Zone and ADAM *is closest.*

> in dangerous territory.
> Spreading ourselves.
> Flexing.
> Muscles jolting.
> We are spasms.
> Bursting out our skin.
> We are alive and armour-plated – we are
> bullet-proof Mossad assassins.

ADAM *is right next to the Red Zone.*

> And one of us is heading for the Red Zone.

REEM *has to shout to be heard – the rest of the group is reaching a climax.*

> Get back. Get away from there. Get away
> from that FUCKING

Then ADAM (*and* ADAM *alone*) *steps into the Red Zone.*
The rest of the group goes silent in a cut-short orgasm.
Pause.
Everyone's terrified – apart from ADAM – *except nothing happens.*

Why's nothing happening, why's

A spotlight turns on, and the rest of the group ducks,
anticipating gunfire – but the gunfire never comes.
The spotlight is shining bright on ADAM.
Then REEM *looks up, whispers:*

It's the bloke off the telly.

SAYEED   What?

REEM   It's Adam Yadin.

SAYEED *looks up.*

SAYEED   What does he want?

ADAM *speaks in* <u>Hebrew</u>:

ADAM   I'm not here to hurt you – do you understand?

REEM   What's he saying?

SAYEED   He's speaking Hebrew.

REEM   SPEAK ARABIC.

ADAM   What?

REEM   ARABIC MOTHERFUCKER.

Now ADAM *speaks in* <u>English</u>:

ADAM   Arabic is no good. English?

REEM   No!

ADAM   But... you are already speaking English?

REEM   I am speaking Arabic.

ADAM   ENGLISH.

REEM   A-RA-BIC.

Pause.

ADAM	Okay. I… am… speaking… Arabic… now.
REEM	Thank you.
SAYEED	You know he's still speaking English?
REEM	No he's not.
ADAM	I speak Arabic.
REEM	You see?
SAYEED	It sounds like English to me.
REEM	Sometimes you aren't half thick Sayeed.

SAYEED *holds up his dictionary, as if proving his point – but* REEM *has already turned to* ADAM.

	What… are… you… doing… here… Adam?
ADAM	I am joining you.
SAYEED	To do what? Brother.
ADAM	To do what you do. We talk about you, in the town, we know what you do.
REEM	So you thought you'd come down here to spy on the Palestinians?
ADAM	No.
REEM	Yes you did Adam.
ADAM	No.
REEM	Then why are you here? –
ADAM	I want to fuck people who killed my daughter.

Big pause.

	Do you understand?
REEM	I understand.

And now everything is focused on ADAM.
The VILLAGERS *gather – they are in formation in front of him – getting closer.*

ADAM   Please don't hurt me.

REEM   Why not?

ADAM   I'm not here to hurt you, I just

REEM   What?

ADAM   I'm

REEM   What, you're what?

ADAM   I don't know.

              –

              I am asking you to back down.

The VILLAGERS *hold back, for a moment, they look at each other.*

The VILLAGERS *rush at* ADAM. *But the second they cross into the Red Zone, gunfire starts.*

Rat-a-tat.

Rounds of lead splatter the stage and quite a few VILLAGERS
fall in ribbons of blood and dust.
Pause. The dust clears.
ADAM *is unharmed. After a while,* REEM *stands – she's
unharmed too. But it looks like* SAYEED *might be fatally
wounded.*

REEM   Sayeed, get up. Get. Up.

And then he gets up. REEM *tends to* SAYEED, *but he shakes
her off.*
SAYEED *wobbles, then straightens up. He touches the big gash
on his head – it hurts.*

              You're going to survive that head wound
              Sayeed.

SAYEED   I will.

REEM   You better. Everyone else is gone.

REEM *gestures around at all the corpses.* SAYEED *nods – he
will stay fatally wounded for the rest of the play – but he'll*

carry on like a trooper, and he'll use pages from his dictionary
to mop up any excess blood.
From the Red Zone, ADAM *coughs.*

        Apart from him. Are you safe over there?

ADAM   I'm sorry about your friends.

REEM   Oh that's very nice of you.

ADAM   But you attacked me.

REEM   Is that right? That's not what I remember.

ADAM   –

REEM   One day I'll stand in there with you, brother.
        You don't believe me, but I will stand right
        next to you.
        I will squeeze my thumbs into your sockets,
        burst your eyeballs, pour bleach into your
        skull, frazzle your brain, suck it out, stamp on
        it, and mash it into thick grainy hummus.
        And it will be very tasty hummus.

ADAM   Well I hope that day never comes.
        –
        Also we invented hummus.

ADAM *runs off,* REEM *and* SAYEED *don't know what to do.*
Pause.
SALWA *drops from the ceiling onto the floor with a SPLAT. She*
lies there for a while, like she's been knocked out.
REEM *and* SAYEED *don't notice her – instead, the pair start*
clearing away the bodies.

SALWA   My fucking head.
        Ammo Sayeed? Ammto Reem? Can you see
        me? Hello?

She tries to stand but immediately falls.

        Oh I'm going to throw up.

She tries to stand again but falls again, dry-retches, then turns
to the audience.

        Can you see me? Can you hear me?

Then back to REEM.

> Ammto, I've been falling for six months.
> I lost.
> I tried getting into the afterlife but when
> I turned up at the gates, they kicked me off
> the cloud and sent me straight back down.
> Which is why you can't fucking see me.
> Hello?
> And I don't know what to do, I guess...
> I need a body.
>
> –
>
> Ammo? Ammto? I need a body.
>
> –
>
> What if you left one of them so I could
> borrow it?
> Please?
> Just one of them, I'm really not picky.

By this point, REEM *and* SAYEED *are back onstage.*

> Ammto Reem?

REEM   Right we've gotta keep going.
            The Intifada doesn't stop, we don't stop.
            And Jawad is – how should I put it? – gaining
            a reputation. He is becoming famous.

SAYEED *checks his dictionary.*

SAYEED   Disreputable. Infamous. Notorious.

REEM   The point is, Sayeed, people only notice
            Palestine when a bomb goes off

A bomb goes off in the distance.

SALWA   It's okay, I can try somewhere else.

REEM   or when the shit hits the fan.
            And the shit is continually hitting the fan.
            Which means we have to take advantage.

SALWA *drags herself off in the direction of the explosion.*

> And Jawad is how we do it – chapter sixteen:
> <u>Palestinian Terrorist Terrorises Innocent
> Soldier</u>

That's the Fox News headline, it's a little bit
one-sided. Al Jazeera's a bit more sober –
chapter sixteen:
Palestinian Teen in Prison Scuffle
Which is fine, but when the Liberal Do-
Gooders report it, they go for clickbait –
chapter sixteen:
An Israeli Soldier has a Loaded Gun But You
Won't Believe What This Brave Palestinian
Does Next!
I promise you that.
You will not believe it.
Jawad has his trial, goes to prison, is spat on,
tries for parole, is spat on some more, and
here we are.
FEBRUARY TWENTY FORTY-FOUR
Intifada in full swing.
Jawad's in court for a hearing – he's up to his
neck in legal aid, campaigns to get him
released.
Cos if nothing else, the do-gooders want to
help.
They always want to help and they always
have the right opinions – bless you, thank you.
And Jawad's in court, cameras rolling,
reporters crammed in, Jawad sidles up to this
soldier, big fella, aggressive type, loaded gun,
Jawad turns to give the cameras a wink, and
then he…

SAYEED   He…?

REEM   YOU WON'T BELIEVE WHAT THIS
            BRAVE PALESTINIAN DOES NEXT

SAYEED   I'm sure I won't.

REEM   He spits. On an armed Israeli soldier. Right on
            his boots.

SAYEED   So?

REEM   So he sticks up for Palestine, he fucks the
            Israelis up.

JAWAD *stands opposite a* SOLDIER.

          Show them how you did it habibi!

JAWAD *doesn't know what to do.*

          Do it baby, spit on him – show them all how
          you spat on that piece of shit!

JAWAD	I… uh
REEM	Come on. You know someone actually made a dance out of it on TikTok. It's quite good.
JAWAD	I was trying to spit on the floor.
REEM	That's not true. Do the spit, do the dance, do the spitting dance.
JAWAD	I was only
REEM	Jawad, habibi, spit on the soldier, okay?
JAWAD	–
REEM	Jawad.
SAYEED	Reem.
REEM	Sayeed.
SAYEED	Leave him.
REEM	I will – when he's shown us how he spat on the soldier.
JAWAD	Mum, I wasn't trying to
REEM	Jawad listen to your mother. Show them.

JAWAD *gathers up spit in his mouth. He watches the*
SOLDIER *then slowly approaches him.* JAWAD *gets ready*
to spit.

SOLDIER	Please. I just polished these boots.
REEM	Ignore the big scary soldier, baby.

After a moment, JAWAD *spits on the* SOLDIER*'s shoe – just a miserable dribble.*
JAWAD *looks up at the* SOLDIER, *terrified.*
And the SOLDIER *lands a great walloping punch on* JAWAD*'s face.*
The SOLDIER *leaves.*
Pause.
REEM *now applies eye make-up to* JAWAD, *so it looks like he has a bruise.*

JAWAD   I'm sorry.

REEM   Don't apologise.
                Sayeed, are you filming this?

SAYEED *does so begrudgingly.*

                Thank you.
                You know, there's a lesson to learn here:
                when life gives you lemons, you've got to
                turn those lemons into shareable content that
                furthers the Palestinian cause.
                There. Done.

She examines JAWAD *and his bruise. She kisses him. Then turns to the audience.*

                When Jawad gets beaten up it is nasty.
                But that's exactly the kind of thing that
                do-gooders love.
                It goes round the world immediately.
                Everyone doing the same spitting-Palestinian
                dance.
                Show them.

JAWAD *does the spitting-Palestinian dance.*

                I love it. Are you posting Sayeed?

Again, SAYEED *does so begrudgingly.*

                Thank you.
                By the way, TikTok doesn't exist in twenty
                forty-four.

SAYEED   That bubble burst very quickly.

REEM	This new app is basically the same, so we're gonna call it TikTok.
	And either way, people are obsessed with Jawad.
JAWAD	They're obsessed with blood and bruises.
REEM	Don't be cynical habibi, that's the state of the world.
	If it bleeds, it leads.
	We can't change that.
SAYEED	But you can still sell Jawad's story.
REEM	We can *tell* his story.
SAYEED	Who to?
REEM	Great question, thank you for asking Sayeed – chapter seventeen:
	<u>Do-Gooder Journalists</u>

JOURNALISTS line up to speak with JAWAD.

JOURNALISTS Mr Hajri, Mr Hajri, Mr Hajri, Mr Hajri!

REEM   Any questions?

There are lots of questions – the JOURNALISTS sometimes speak in chorus, sometimes speak separately.

Make them good questions!

As the questions keep piling up JAWAD is photographed.

JOURNALISTS Mr Hajri, do you consider yourself a fighter?
Mr Hajri, what makes a hero?
Why does everyone love an anti-hero, Mr Hajri?
Mr Hajri, your story is so important.
My Hajri, can you do the dance?
Mr Hajri, you're so savage, yet so noble.
Mr Hajri, why are you so handsome?
Mr Hajri, do the sands of Arabia invigorate your blood?
Your eyes are so brown.
So brooding and Arab.

Mr Hajri, what do you think are the chances
of a Palestinian state?
Mr Hajri, you're so scary and sexy.
Mr Hajri, why are the Israelis so mean to you?
Tell us your gritty life story, Mr Hajri.
Why are the Israelis so nasty?
Tell us your story.
Make it a little bit scary, a little bit sexy.
From the dusts of Arabia.
What about the evil Israelis?
Spit on them!
What about the poor Palestinians!
Do the dance!
And can you be topless?
With bulging Arabian muscles!
All dead gritty.
Scary and sexy.
Show us.
Show us.
So noble, so savage.
Yeah!
Tell us.
Tell us.

Unnoticed and undercover, ADAM *has appeared, dressed as
a journalist.*

ADAM   Tell us about Sara Yadin.

                Silence – REEM *steps forward.*

REEM   Excuse me?

JOURNALISTS –

REEM   Which one of you said that?

The JOURNALISTS *step to one side and exit – this leaves*
ADAM *standing alone.*

ADAM   I did.

REEM   Why are you asking?

ADAM   Because he murdered her.

REEM	I see.
ADAM	Well?
	–
REEM	In the last one hundred and six days, do you know how many Israelis have died?
ADAM	Six.
REEM	And how many Palestinians?
ADAM	–
REEM	One thousand two hundred and forty-seven.

Gunshot.

> One thousand two hundred and forty-eight.
> Against six.
> Is anyone else hearing that number? Is anyone else furious about that number?
> Look.
> I'm not saying it's a competition, but also –
> chapter eighteen:
> DEATH-TOLL COMPETITION
> WOOOOOOOO! Are you ready?

No response.

> I said: WOOOOOOOO! Are you ready?

No response. Then REEM *walks offstage.*

| SAYEED | Reem? Reem. |

With REEM *gone,* SAYEED *doesn't know what to do.*

> Ahem.
> In times of conflict, the unequal death tolls of Israelis and Palestinians are frequently politicised and manipulated, in order to condemn the disproportionate response of the Israeli military.
> And I happen to think it is a sad state of affairs that the loss of human life is taken advantage of so shamelessly. It is tasteless.

REEM has reappeared with a wheelbarrow.

REEM   Absolutely right.

SAYEED   Really?

REEM   The problem is, I very much enjoy
              politicising and manipulating the unequal
              death tolls of Israelis and Palestinians, in
              order to condemn the disproportionate
              response of the Israeli military.
              Because fuck the Israeli military.

She tips the wheelbarrow out: one thousand, two hundred and forty-eight figurines fall out into a large pile.

              This is what one thousand two hundred and
              forty-eight dead bodies looks like.

Then she reaches into her pocket.

              This is what six dead bodies looks like.

And holds out six dead bodies in her hand.
Meanwhile – unnoticed – SALWA comes on, looking for a dead body to occupy.
She digs through the pile, efficiently examining and discarding the bodies.

              Can you tell the difference?
              I'm just trying to put this into perspective.
              Sara Yadin accounts for sixteen-point-six-per-
              cent of Israeli deaths.
              Salwa Hajri accounts for nought-point-
              nought-eight-per-cent of Palestinian deaths.
              For every Sara Yadin there are two hundred
              and eight Salwa Hajris.
              In terms of the raw figures we crush the
              Israelis.
              We are undefeated and unassailable.

ADAM   It's more complicated than that.

REEM   Is it? What, are you going to start telling me
              you have a 'stronger defence force'. That you
              have a more organised army, more long-
              distance missiles, less dense population

centres, more efficient military tactics, more
access to military resources, soldiers, that
you're just better at keeping civilian
casualties to a minimum?

ADAM   No.

REEM   Or maybe you'll go off on one about human
            shields

ADAM   No.

REEM   some bollocks about how we're responsible
            for killing our own people, is that it?

SAYEED   He said no.

REEM *scoffs*. ADAM *gives up and leaves*.

REEM   I don't give a shit what he's got to say.
            C'mon, you can clear this up now.

SAYEED   Already?

REEM   Yes.

SAYEED   You made all this mess just for that?

REEM   Yes! It's an important point Sayeed, I'm not
            pissing about.

SALWA   You can get rid of them all by the way, none
            of them are any use.

REEM   Go on then.

SAYEED   Why me?

REEM   I've got to do the next bit.

SAYEED   –

REEM   Thank you habibi.

SAYEED *clears away the figurines*.
SALWA *watches him*.
REEM *turns to the audience*.

            This is the bit where everyone gives me
            a cheer.

For Salwa.
Because I don't think nought-point-nought-
eight per cent is reflective of her contribution
to this fight.
C'mon, give me a cheer.

Alone and unheard, SALWA *does a little cheer.*

I can't hear you. I want a PROPER CHEER.

Again: SALWA *does a little cheer.*

For Palestine because Palestine is winning
and Palestine will keep winning.
It is one hell of a competition and it is the best
prize of them all:
The High-Horse Prize for Highest Number of
Casualties – chapter nineteen:
<u>PALESTINE IS STILL FUCKING
WINNING</u>

Then REEM *sits.*
SAYEED *is opposite her.*

SAYEED	Are you alright?
REEM	I'm fine.
SAYEED	You can be honest with me.
REEM	I'm telling you I'm fine Sayeed so let's leave it.
SAYEED	–
REEM	Why shouldn't I be fine?
SAYEED	I, uh, I dunno.
REEM	Course you don't.
SAYEED	What does that mean?
REEM	Means you're indecisive Sayeed. Means it doesn't matter whether I'm fine, or you're fine, or if anyone's fine, or alive, or dead, it doesn't matter because what matters is Palestine.
SAYEED	Okay.

REEM	It means you're asking a stupid question. –
SAYEED	Well I'm sorry.
REEM	For what?
SAYEED	Just. That we even live here.
REEM	Yeah, I'm sorry about that too but it's not gonna change any time soon. –
SAYEED	Can you imagine what it'd be like, not living here? Not doing all of this?
REEM	Doing what?
SAYEED	All of it. Protests and campaigns and watching people die and Imagine just not doing it.
REEM	What, like being dead?
SAYEED	No, like living somewhere else. Can you imagine that?
REEM	No.
SAYEED	I can – every day. I imagine peeling an orange and pretending that it's actually just a bit of fruit – not some Israeli commodity that we can't boycott because we need to eat.
REEM	That's what you actually think about?
SAYEED	Sometimes. Mostly I wish I lived in a penthouse in Dubai.
REEM	Why do you want to live in Dubai?
SAYEED	Point is, I want to be a billionaire, Reem. Point is, this place won't change, and I want money, and if I've got money then I can be done with all this, I can be gone.

REEM	–
SAYEED	With you.
REEM	Oh thank you.
SAYEED	Obviously with you.
REEM	You know what I want?
SAYEED	You want this to be over.
REEM	I want it to be finished. Properly. I want this place to change.

REEM *stands. She walks over to the Red Zone.*

SAYEED   Reem? Reem.

But she doesn't stop, she keeps walking, and she steps into the Red Zone.
Nothing happens, REEM *looks around.*

REEM   Maybe it can change. And maybe I can change it.

Then a shot is fired – but REEM *dodges the bullet.*
She stands up straight, in shock.
Then a huge grin spreads over her face.

SAYEED   Please get out of there. Please.

Another shot fired, she dodges it again, confident this time, her smile is smug.
REEM *steps out.*

REEM   That's a true story by the way, I fuck you not: I dodged two bullets.
          I went into the Red Zone and I dodged two bullets.
          Like it was nothing.
          Like I demand something and it just happens – chapter twenty:
          <u>What Reem Demands</u>
          Jawad spits on the soldier.
          He gets beaten up.
          Protests get more violent, more Palestinians are dead.

But I demand one thing: I demand that Jawad
is released.
And you know what…?
My demand is met.
Surprise motherfuckers!
JUNE TWENTY FORTY-FIVE
Ceasefire.
No more Palestinian rockets, no more
kidnappings, no more protests.
In exchange for the release of Jawad Hajri.

She clicks her fingers.
And JAWAD *appears – he's got sunglasses on.*

Who's been missed. So much.

She looks at her son, smiles at him. Then JAWAD *removes the*
sunglasses to reveal the bruise. REEM *hugs her son.*

By the way he now has a hundred and twelve
thousand TikTok followers.

JAWAD   A hundred and thirteen – it keeps going up.

SAYEED   We're very proud of him.

REEM   Don't take the piss. Jawad is the subject of
a momentous agreement.
The Israelis have their hands tied because the
journalists have published too many stories.
And we have thrown too many stones.
Peace is inevitable.
It's a big day, it's a celebration: Jawad Hajri is
released and we cheer for him.
Because he is adored.
Because he is invincible.

SAYEED   Because he's a brat.

JAWAD   Oi!

SAYEED   And you know what happens next?

JAWAD   What?

SAYEED   They can't do anything. The pair of them.

JAWAD *and* REEM *are now sat – they are bored.*

> Itching out their skin, thinking they can take
> on the world, they can do nothing.

REEM   Whatever Sayeed.

SAYEED   They have agreed to a ceasefire.
              And the terms of this are not:
              Ceasefire, apart from Jawad and Reem who
              are allowed to start protests and chuck rocks
              at soldiers.
              No.
              The terms are:
              We give you Jawad Hajri, you give us
              obedience.
              Which you won't admit, Reem, and Jawad
              won't admit it, and Jawad's followers

JAWAD   A hundred and twenty-eight thousand

SAYEED   certainly won't say it.
              They'll all tell you we beat them down, but
              I'll tell you the truth:
              We gave up. Because things *never* change.
              Which is fine by me, it's not my problem but
              we gave up.
              I advocate giving up, by the way.
              We're not gonna win, so let's stop sending
              thousands of Palestinians to their deaths for
              the hell of it.

JAWAD*'s tapping his foot.* REEM*'s drumming her fingers.*
Spotlight and SAYEED *turns to the audience.*

> Reem lost a daughter.
> And that means I lost a daughter.
> She was called Loubna.
> She *is* called Loubna because her spirit is
> eternal even if her body is maggots – chapter
> twenty-one:
> <u>My Turn</u>
> In early twenty forty-two, I headed a protest
> which ended up at the al-Aqsa mosque.

It became violent, deaths on both sides, and
I was targeted as a member of an 'extremist
faction' of the Palestinian community.
It was a protest against an import tariff on
oranges.
I am a man who sells fruit and vegetables.
But the IDF come to our house anyway.
The tank pulled up round the back and the
Israeli soldiers climbed onto it to hop the
garden wall.
Another soldier knocked on the front door to
distract us.
Knock knock.
Who's there?
Sara Yadin.
Jawad was out, I was out. Reem was at home.
Loubna was out back.
–

Reem was cooking lentils, she turned the gas
down, went to to the front door, answered the
knock.
Sara Yadin was there.
She was a distraction.
And Loubna stayed out back and the soldiers,
who hopped the garden wall, used rifles.
They had intelligence that I was at home, but
I wasn't.
They fired anyway.
We know Sara's name cos she held up her ID
at the front door and acted like it was nothing
so Reem didn't get suspicious.
It was a stupid thing to do cos the name Sara
Yadin stuck in Reem's head, stuck in my
head, stuck in Jawad's head and now we're
here.
–

And we never say the name 'Sara Yadin' – it
just lingers. Like a moist fart.
No, that's a lie: we have spoken about Sara
Yadin once.

Me and Reem and Jawad. Once, watching
telly. I go: *Reem, we should talk.*
And she goes: *About what?*
And I say: *That time she came to the door,
when Loubna*
And I can't finish the sentence so she says:
Maybe. She shrugs.
Jawad turns *Arab Idol* up.
And maybe it's all for the worst or the best.
Or maybe we get what we deserve.
Maybe we've got to fight.
Maybe we need to strike oil and become Gulfi
billionaires... I don't know.
July twenty forty-five.

REEM   Oi.

SAYEED   What?

REEM   Twat-face.

SAYEED   Don't call me that.

REEM   I'm the one who shouts out dates.

SAYEED   Not now you don't. July twenty forty-five

REEM   And what happens in July twenty forty-five?

SAYEED   Nothing.
              AUGUST TWENTY FORTY-FIVE
              More nothing.
              Not even protests, not even dogging, and we
              love dogging, but the spark is gone.
              Same with September.
              Same with October.
              Nothing, again and again and it is shit.

Pause.

REEM   Thank you for that Sayeed.

SAYEED   I'm not finished.

REEM   Oh really?

SAYEED   Yes, because Sara Yadin knocked on our door
              for a reason.

REEM	To kill my daughter.
SAYEED	Our daughter. And no, no, she was
REEM	What?
SAYEED	She was enlisted, she was
REEM	So?
SAYEED	So she was
REEM	What, Sayeed? –
SAYEED	Wait here.

SAYEED runs off. After a moment, he comes back on with ADAM.

REEM	What's he doing here?
SAYEED	Listen to him.
REEM	No.
SAYEED	Just listen – chapter twenty-two:

But REEM *puts fingers in her ears.*

REEM	LA LA LA LA LA LA LA LA LA LA LA LA
SAYEED	Chapter twenty-two
REEM	LA LA LA LA LA LA LA LA LA LA LA LA
SAYEED	Reem.
REEM	I'M NOT LISTENING
SAYEED	Reem, I am sick of pretending Sara Yadin is the most evil person on the planet when
REEM	When what?
SAYEED	I thought you weren't listening.
REEM	When what?

Beat.

SAYEED	Me and Adam, we are both fathers – who have lost daughters.
REEM	Ugh.
SAYEED	Don't dismiss that.
REEM	Then don't be so wet, Sayeed. *Fathers who have lost daughters.* You lost – *we* lost – an innocent twelve-year-old, shot in the head at point-blank range. What did he lose?
SAYEED	A daughter.
REEM	A soldier. Who fought for an army that spends every single day making our lives hell. Choking us.
SAYEED	I know.
REEM	So you'll also know that choices have consequences. Right?
SAYEED	Sara didn't choose to be in that position.
REEM	She had more of a choice than Loubna.

Pause.

| SAYEED | Chapter twenty-two:
<u>Adam</u> |

ADAM *is now opposite* REEM. *They look at each other.*

| | Speak. Adam. |
| ADAM | What I believe is everyone deserves a context. And I know I'm biased but I am going to give us a context.
Sara was a soldier because she was conscripted – by law – she was eighteen.
And I was a soldier because I was conscripted.
And I remained a soldier – afterwards – because it was a living, because there were no other options. |

	I was a kitchen supervisor in the maintenance corps. I started out cooking lentils. And Sara Sara was going to leave the army as soon as she could.

REEM   So what?

ADAM   So on her first day, Sara was sent to a Palestinian house, told to hold up her ID while soldiers went round the back, fired, by accident, and killed a twelve-year-old girl.

Quiet.

REEM   It wasn't an accident.

ADAM   I only know what I heard.

REEM   I know because I was there.

ADAM   You saw it happen?

REEM   I saw no one was charged.

ADAM   There was an investigation.

REEM   And what did that achieve?

ADAM   –

REEM   So whose daughter matters more?

ADAM   Mine.
If we're talking about the law. Politics. Security. Access to education, healthcare, work, transport.
Land.
A home.
–

REEM   You just have to see whose home is riddled with bullets.

ADAM   I've been shot at by Palestinians.

REEM   What, they threw a few rocks?

ADAM   My home is covered in barbed wire.
                My town is surrounded by it.
                Guards.
                Patrols.
                In case you

REEM   What?

ADAM   In case you attack.

REEM   In case we take back what is ours.
                –

ADAM   We pay our rent.

REEM   Ha!

ADAM   And our town is the only place where I can
                afford the rent. So where else do we go?

REEM   Oh I'm not getting into this.

ADAM   So it's fine to sit back and criticise when
                you've got money.
                It is easy to have morals when you have
                money or you live in some far-off country or
                in Tel Aviv
                But we do not have money.

ADAM *looks at* REEM.

                Are you listening?
                I fought because my grandmother told me
                stories about fleeing Europe.
                I fought because my grandmother told me
                stories about how the Arabs kept trying to
                invade us.
                And, yes, they invaded us because we
                attacked them.
                But we attacked them because they blew us up.
                And they blew us up because the British
                supported us.
                And the British supported us because we blew
                them up.
                And we blew them up because they attacked us.

And they attacked us because we were
fighting them.
Is this making sense?
Because we were fighting them because they
were fighting us.
And before that, we fought them.
And before that, they fought us.
And before that, before we fought them, and
they fought us, there were the Ottomans.
Who loved a fight.
And then the Mamluks.
And the Ayyubids.
And they were fighting off the British – again
– because they started a crusade.
To get rid of the caliphate.
Which replaced the Byzantines.
Which replaced the Romans.
Which replaced the Greeks.
And who can forget the Assyrians?
And the Babylonians.
And the Israelites.
And the Philistines.
Who fought us because we fought them.
And if I trace it back, I was a soldier because
my great-great-great-great-great-great-great-
great-great-great-great-great-great-great-
great-great-great-great-great-great-great-
grandfather got hit by a rock.
And he wanted revenge, so he threw a rock.
At his neighbour.
And his neighbour fought back.
And then he fought back.
And then he fought back.
And it *was* mostly men.
And they kept fighting and fighting and
fighting and fighting and fighting and fighting.

REEM *looks at* ADAM.

REEM   Is that it?

SAYEED   He's barely started.

REEM	Oh I'm sure he hasn't.
ADAM	No I think that sums it up.
	–

REEM	Except the problem, Sayeed, is that the context for Sara turning up at our door is not Adam Yadin. It is not the history of the fucking world. It is you – starting a protest. They looked for you, they didn't find you, and instead they found my daughter. And you have never had an answer to that.

SAYEED	–

REEM	Have you?

SAYEED *still doesn't have an answer. It's a little awkward.*

ADAM	Ahem. I should go.
REEM	I think you should, Adam.
SAYEED	And I might nip off too.
REEM	Sayeed.

ADAM *leaves. But of course* SAYEED *doesn't. He thinks.*

SAYEED	Maybe there isn't an answer.

REEM	Yes there is. And you keep saying *I'm* the one who doesn't talk about Loubna, but I try. I *want* to talk about her. But the conversation ends because you do not have a response, or an apology, or an answer to the fact that they were searching for you. And shot her.

Pause.

SAYEED	I was out buying sugar. I needed sugar for tea and while I was out they, they, they came and they…

REEM   Oh stop it Sayeed, it's exhausting. It is so
                fucking boring listening to the words come
                out of your mouth, when you spend more
                time making excuses for yourself than
                fighting for *us*.

SAYEED *starts walking off.* REEM *holds up the dictionary.*

                You're forgetting your dictionary.

SAYEED   Keep it.

REEM   But how will you know how to define *useless
                coward*?!

SAYEED   –

REEM   It's no use walking off Sayeed, we've got an
                Intifada to win.

SAYEED   What Intifada?

SAYEED *goes.* REEM *throws the dictionary at him.*
And then she's alone.
She straightens herself out.
And then she starts cooking.
It is a normal, quiet, afternoon.

REEM   Chapter twenty-three:
                <u>Reem Cooks Lentils</u>
                God that is a boring title.

*She keeps cooking, for a while… then there's a knock at the
door.* REEM *ignores it.*
After a moment, another knock.
REEM *stops stirring, turns the gas down, moves towards the
front door.*

                Loubna? Come in from the garden habibti.

Another knock.

                I'm not opening the door.

Nothing. Then another knock.

                Sara. Do you hear? I am not opening that door.

Then JAWAD *appears behind* REEM.

JAWAD	Mum?
REEM	Jawad. What are you doing?
JAWAD	Nothing, sorry, I just… I saw Tariq.
REEM	What?
JAWAD	Tariq, cousin Tariq. I saw him.
REEM	How?
JAWAD	This morning – out near the settlement.
REEM	You shouldn't be out there.
JAWAD	No one noticed.
REEM	Where was he?
JAWAD	Still on the roof.
REEM	What?
JAWAD	He's still caught on the roof, his skin looked green.
REEM	They didn't remove the body?
JAWAD	Well, no. Because he's alive. Sort of. It's been two years so he's calcified. Like a statue. But he's there, he blinks and he calls out, he asks for food.
REEM	And does anyone give him food?
JAWAD	I don't know. I couldn't get close enough, you have to pay to see him.
REEM	–
JAWAD	He's like a tourist attraction: they've sectioned it off, the Palestinians are protesting outside and the do-gooders pay to go inside.

REEM   To do what?

JAWAD   To mourn him. They've come from all over
              the world to mourn him.

Sad music starts playing.
The DO-GOODERS *line up, handkerchiefs at the ready.*
TARIQ, *calcified and grey, is in position, caught in barbed*
wire, stuck on the roof.

REEM   I don't understand.

JAWAD   And it's not just Israelis, foreigners as well.
              They pay for an authentic guide who'll show
              them the authentic West Bank.
              And they all take photos and pictures and
              follow guides with little red umbrellas.
              And there are people selling embroidered
              handkerchiefs – little Palestinian flag in the
              corner – which you buy at the door.
              Then you walk inside to see Tariq, except
              they don't call him Tariq.
              They call him: The Fallen Palestinian.
              There's sad music and everything, and you
              mop up your tears with a handkerchief.

The DO-GOODERS *are crying, taking photos, eating crisps,*
taking photos, crying.

TARIQ   Does anyone have any food…? Anyone…?

The crying continues. But no one hears him.

JAWAD   I left cos one kid was trying to chuck a rock
              and the crowd was getting riled up.

REEM   You didn't help him?

JAWAD   What am I gonna do? He stays there, he's alive
              – better than being added to the death toll.
              At least this way the Israelis are protecting
              him not trying to shoot him dead.

REEM   They want him dead anyway.

JAWAD   You reckon?

REEM	They all do.
JAWAD	See I reckon if something happened to Tariq they'd have a riot on their hands. They'd have another Intifada. And not even they want that.

Pause.

	Lentils smell good.
REEM	I'm so bored of these fucking lentils.
TARIQ	Anyone spare any food…?
REEM	Bin them.

REEM *hands the lentils to* JAWAD – JAWAD *throws them in the bin.*
After a moment, REEM *moves towards* TARIQ.
She picks up SAYEED*'s dictionary, weighs it in her hand – then creeps up on* TARIQ, *lifting the book above her head.*
She watches TARIQ… *and she's about to bring the book down on his head when:*

TARIQ	Ammto Reem?
REEM	Tariq.
TARIQ	What are you doing here?
REEM	Nothing. Nothing. How are you?
TARIQ	I'm fine… what's that in your hand?

REEM *drops the dictionary.*

REEM	That? Nothing. Ignore it. I was, um, I'm just here to bring you food.
TARIQ	You have food?
REEM	Well. No. I forgot the food.
TARIQ	Oh.
REEM	But I've come to help.
TARIQ	Great.

REEM   –

TARIQ   How are you going to help?

Pause. REEM *looks at* TARIQ.

REEM   We've missed you Tariq.

Subtly, she picks up the dictionary.

               All of us.

TARIQ   What's going on?

REEM   Nothing, you shouldn't panic.

TARIQ   I'm not panicking, I'm confused.

REEM   We're all confused, Tariq.
               It's just the world we live in now.

TARIQ   Ammto Reem?

She approaches TARIQ.
Unnoticed, SAYEED *is onstage.*

               I don't know what you're doing but I'm
               scared.

REEM   You shouldn't be.

TARIQ   But I am.

REEM   I'm taking you away from this place.

TARIQ   I like it here.

REEM   No you don't.

TARIQ   It's safe, there's a good view.

REEM   But no one wants to be here. Not really. Not
               actually.

SAYEED   Reem?

REEM *turns to him.*

               What are you doing?

Pause.

REEM	I don't know.
SAYEED	Why don't you give me the dictionary?
REEM	No.
SAYEED	That's okay. Then why don't you step down from there?
REEM	I like it up here.
SAYEED	But I think you should leave Tariq alone. Hi Tariq.
TARIQ	Hey Ammo.
REEM	I'm not concerned with what you think.
SAYEED	Reem.
REEM	I thought you'd gone – but you always manage to turn up at the exact wrong moment.
SAYEED	The moment you're about to kill Tariq?
TARIQ	Excuse me?
REEM	Sayeed, I don't know what's in your head but you are misinterpreting whatever it is you think you've seen.
SAYEED	I think you're making a mistake.
REEM	No I'm not.
SAYEED	Yes you are – and I recognise a mistake when I see it.
REEM	Because you've made enough of them.
SAYEED	Exactly.
REEM	–
SAYEED	And I would like to stop making them – I would like you to stop making them. Step away from him.
REEM	No.

SAYEED   Step away.

Pause.

REEM   I guess we're at an impasse.

REEM *holds up the dictionary.*

Do you want me to look that up for you?

Then the lights flicker – TARIQ looks up.

Or do you just want to keep telling me off?

There's the whistle of something from above.

TARIQ   Oh no. No. Can anyone hear that?

REEM   Or do you want to keep guilt-tripping me?

SAYEED   It's not a guilt-trip.

REEM   You're right – it would be a guilt-trip if it
                      actually worked.

The whistle is getting closer.

Because your mistakes are not my mistakes.

SAYEED   Don't say that.

REEM   They are your shit to deal with.

And closer…

TARIQ   Can anyone hear that drone? Hello? Hello?

REEM   Because I am fighting better and fighting
                      harder and I will not spend my life fucking up
                      and feeling guilty and then fucking up some
                      more.

TARIQ   Help me, please. Someone. Please. Please.
                      HELP.

Until there's a drone strike. Rubble everywhere.
And in the chaos:

REEM   FEBRUARY TWENTY FORTY-SIX
                      The deadlock is over.

Peace gets snapped and I don't even bludgeon
anyone to death with a dictionary!
It is brilliant!
I mean it's terrible!
See, the Americans are trying to push through
peace talks.
And the peace talks are going swimmingly.

SAYEED   Are they?

REEM   Of course not! When have peace talks ever
gone well?!
We don't like it. So we get angry and a scuffle
breaks out somewhere in the north, and then
there's a retaliation, and suddenly BAM –
chapter twenty-four:
The Intifada Stops for No One
Beit al-Qadir is turned to rubble in a huge
drone strike – but who cares?!
We've got our fight back. And you don't need
a roof over your head when you've got fight.

SAYEED   Yes you do.

REEM   Piss off Sayeed.
The Intifada is back. The protests are back.
The resistance is back.
I feel alive.
And we are going to put Palestine on the map.
Literally.

REEM *runs off.*

SAYEED   You know you shouldn't get overexcited
about all this... Reem?

And REEM *strolls back on with a huge bazooka.*

Oh Jesus Christ.

She aims it at SAYEED – *who ducks. Then* REEM *lowers it.*

REEM   Your face! I'm not gonna shoot you.

SAYEED   What are you doing with that?

REEM	I'm livening things up, I'm showing that I'm dead serious this time.
SAYEED	About what?
REEM	About butchering our enemies.
SAYEED	Reem!
REEM	Joke! I am not butchering anyone.

JAWAD *enters, also with bazooka.*

> I mean, it's mostly self-defence – we've got a village to protect.

SAYEED	Our village is rubble.
REEM	Well me and my son happen to be very fond of this rubble.

JAWAD *and* REEM *put on sunglasses, they look bad-ass, they are the stars of their own action movie.*

SOLDIERS *enter.*

JAWAD *and* REEM *look at each other, nod, then blast the* SOLDIERS *away.*

More SOLDIERS.

Who JAWAD *and* REEM *blast away.*

SAYEED *stands in the middle of it all.*

More SOLDIERS.

Who JAWAD *and* REEM *blast away.*

It takes a few attempts for SAYEED*'s voice to be heard…*

SAYEED   This isn't what happens.

More SOLDIERS.

> This isn't what happens.

Who JAWAD *and* REEM *blast away.*

> This isn't what happens.

More SOLDIERS.

THIS ISN'T WHAT HAPPENS.

JAWAD *and* REEM *try to fire but the bazookas don't work. They try again. Still doesn't work. They make the sound of their bazookas firing… but it fizzles out.*

REEM   Die. Scum. Die…

The SOLDIERS *just stare at* REEM *and* JAWAD.

                Shit.

SAYEED   Chapter twenty-five:
                The Bazookas Aren't Real
                Obviously.
                My wife does not have access to bazookas.
                What she does have is a semi-famous son.

JAWAD   A hundred and forty-six thousand on TikTok.

SAYEED   Who the soldiers recognise.

JAWAD   A hundred and sixty-three thousand.

SAYEED   And aren't too happy with.

JAWAD   A hundred and eighty-five thousand.

SAYEED   THIS IS WHAT ACTUALLY HAPPENS.

ADAM *takes over.*

ADAM   There are two protests taking place.
                I am placed at the front of one.
                Jawad Hajri is placed at the front of another.
                I follow him on TikTok.
                He dances a lot.
                It's a funny thing to do for a boy who killed
                my daughter.
                When the two protests meet, they become
                a riot and the soldiers rain down on him.
                He runs.
                I watch him running towards me.
                He's got bleached eyes that stare at me.
                He registers nothing.

> Doesn't know where or how he's running.
> Eyes are lead, legs in a blur.
> Heading on to Israeli territory.
> He crosses the divide and lights spark up.
> Searchlights. Sirens. He keeps running.
> It is not my job to get involved.
> I stick my foot out.
> The toe of my boot catches his shin and he
> lands in mud, ten feet away.
> I feel bad.
> And I don't.
> And I watch as he squirms.
> That's what happens.

VILLAGERS *are onstage – their voices are soft, far away.*
JAWAD *is led away.*
REEM *watches on.*

> Most of the Palestinians are stuck fighting and
> swearing at the Israelis.
> Most of the Palestinians are being beaten.

VILLAGERS   FREE
              FREE
              PALESTINE

ADAM   I watch a group of soldiers lift Jawad's body.
              He's placed in a van.

VILLAGERS   FREE
              FREE
              PALESTINE

ADAM   The van slips off and the protest is such
              a mess that no one notices.
              The van doesn't head to the station.
              The van heads in the opposite direction.

REEM *emerges from the group of* VILLAGERS *– the chant
trails off.*

> The complete opposite direction.

SAYEED *finds his dictionary on the ground. It's bloody and
torn and he tries repairing it.*

REEM	Chapter twenty-six: <u>We Keep Fighting</u>
SAYEED	That's not what we do.
REEM	We keep fighting.
SAYEED	'To endeavour vigorously to win.' That is not what we are capable of doing.
REEM	So what are we doing?
SAYEED	We are failing to win – that's what we're doing – chapter twenty-six: <u>We Keep Losing</u> Or, you know what, maybe we already have failed – chapter twenty-six: <u>We Are Lost</u>

Quiet.
SAYEED *puts his dictionary away. He takes a phone from his pocket, and holds it out for* REEM.
ADAM *stands behind* SAYEED.

	I think you should look at this.
REEM	What is it?
SAYEED	–
REEM	Where's Jawad, where's he gone?
SAYEED	He's been arrested.
REEM	So are we going down to the station?
SAYEED	Reem.
REEM	Make sure they treat him right – diligence and due process and justice, we can start a campaign and
SAYEED	–
REEM	Why are you looking at me like that?
SAYEED	I'm not.
REEM	Except there's a look on your face like shat-on bedsheets.

SAYEED	–
REEM	It means that look needs wiping off – tell me what's going on.
SAYEED	Jawad isn't at the station.
REEM	So where is he?
SAYEED	–
REEM	Is that why you're showing me the phone?
SAYEED	Yes.
REEM	What if I don't want to look?

REEM *doesn't take the phone.*

SAYEED	Just watch it. Please.
REEM	Are you going to watch it?
SAYEED	–
REEM	Because I don't want to watch this alone.
SAYEED	–
REEM	Will you? Sayeed, I am asking if you'll
SAYEED	–
REEM	Sayeed?
SAYEED	–
REEM	Okay I want to be honest with you. And that means I need to tell you that Sayeed is dead. He died. When we went dogging after the interval. Which is typical of him, so embarrassing, but it's what happened. He fell down, he never got up – chapter twenty-seven:
	–
	And I wanted him to get up so badly. But no one survives that wound.

As REEM *speaks,* SAYEED *slowly lies down on the floor and twists his limbs so it looks like he's dead.*

> The tip of the bullet is perforated and his skull cracked on impact.
> The exit wound was two inches wider than the entry wound which implies that the bullet burst open the moment it hit his flesh.
> His brain turned to grainy hummus and he was dead before he noticed it.
> Twat.
> He never notices a thing.

ADAM *has taken the phone from* SAYEED*'s hand. He has walked over to* REEM *– and now he hands her the phone.*

> What I watch – alone – is
> It's a livestream.
> It lasts eighty-three seconds.
> It is filmed in the same basement where Sara was killed.

She watches the phone – REEM *is only lit by the glow of the screen.*
ADAM *retreats.*

> Everyone watches, all of Palestine.
> And if Jawad Hajri wasn't my son, I'd…
> And if Sayeed was here, he'd…
> I don't know.
> Maybe he'd tell me to, um

Now VILLAGERS *come and gather round the screen – a different* VILLAGER *takes each line.*

VILLAGERS   To watch.

REEM   Yeah.

VILLAGERS   Cos when the livestream begins, Jawad's already covered in petrol.
             He's being held close to a naked flame.
             Too close.
             And it's a soldier who holds the match, holds it far away, close, far away.
             We can't see Jawad's tears for the petrol.

REEM	His face is scrunched... gravel.
VILLAGERS	Close, far away then the match burns out.
	Someone fumbles with the phone, camera
	whizzes past green soldier uniforms.
	Someone lights another match and the image
	refocuses and
	Close, far away, close, far away, then really
	close.
	Should-be-on-fire close.
REEM	It's silent.
VILLAGERS	Pin drop.
	Close, far away.
	They're not gonna do it.
	Close, far away.
	They won't.
	Close, far away.
	But the match burns down.
	The flame licks the soldier's hand.
	Close, far away.
	Thumb and forefinger.
	Which gets caught in the flame.
	His skin.
	And the sound is cracked – we hear the
	soldier swear in Hebrew, we see him
REEM	Let go of the match.
	And the flame it, it jumps...
	Onto, onto, onto, onto
VILLAGERS	Onto Jawad.
REEM	–
VILLAGERS	And Jawad's face
REEM	Disappears because the Wi-Fi cuts.
	–
	I wait for Sayeed to speak.
	Wait for him to say
	What happens next?
	He doesn't.
	So I say

Let's turn the Wi-Fi off and on again.

And I wait for Sayeed to say

Reem, the electricity's cut, that's not gonna work.

Which, again, he doesn't.
So I say

Let's wait.

REEM *waits*.

VILLAGERS   And as Reem waits, different versions of her
               future stretch out.

REEM   Please don't speak.

VILLAGERS   Versions that could exist.

REEM   Please.

VILLAGERS   Where she screams.
               Or cries.
               Is furious.
               Throws a fit.
               Is completely still.

REEM   Stop speaking.

VILLAGERS   She does everything.
               Demands justice.
               Buys a gun.
               Demands revenge.
               Calls the press.
               Demands that we remember.

REEM   Please stop.
               –

VILLAGERS   Or she gets swallowed up.

REEM   Stop it.
               And if you could, could fuck off. Please. Cos
               I'm trying to…

The VILLAGERS *leave.*
After a while, REEM *tries speaking. She finds* SAYEED*'s*
dictionary and picks it up. She flicks through it: nothing.
It's a long time before words form.

make sense.

–

But I don't know if

–

I don't know, I

–

Cos Jawad is still…

–

Chapter twenty-eight:
<u>Jawad is Still…</u>

The light from the phone screen cuts out.
We're in a basement, barely lit.
There's a pile of ashes on the floor.
JAWAD *enters and stares at the pile of ashes.*
After a while, SALWA *enters.*
She stands next to JAWAD*, also staring at the pile of ashes.*

SALWA   Is that…?

JAWAD   Yup.

SALWA   Shit.

Pause.

Maybe you shouldn't have dropped that
cinder block.

JAWAD   What?

SALWA   I'm just saying, we wouldn't be in this mess if
it wasn't for you.

JAWAD   Me? What about you?

SALWA   What did I do?

JAWAD   You were there.

SALWA   You're the one who dropped the cinder block!

JAWAD	Only cos you told me to.
SALWA	I didn't.
JAWAD	But you nodded.
SALWA	Fuck off, did I nod.
JAWAD	You nodded. So I dropped it. It's not my fault.
SALWA	What are you talking about?
JAWAD	It's what happened, Salwa, it's the truth.
SALWA	You need your head examined, if that's what you think
JAWAD	Well maybe you need
SALWA	What?

Then TARIQ *is there.*

TARIQ	Hello?

He moves over to the others and is about to speak when:

JAWAD	Don't.
TARIQ	Right.

TARIQ *sees the pile of ashes.*
Now they all stare at it.

JAWAD	We just need to find another body.
TARIQ	Exactly.
SALWA	Yeah.

Suddenly, SARA *drops from the ceiling on to the floor with a SPLAT.*
She stands, dazed, and looks at the others.
They look at her.

JAWAD	Why are you here?
SARA	They didn't let me in.
SALWA	Why?
SARA	You can only get in with your own body.

This sinks in.

SALWA   No one told me this is what happens after we
               die.

SARA   Me neither.

TARIQ   Or me.

JAWAD   Or me.

Pause.
ADAM *is onstage.*

ADAM   Epilogue:
               One Israeli Goes Dogging
               Not to fuck the Palestinians, but because he
               likes it.
               We Israelis get turned on by the risk.

ADAM *is alone now. In the background, a* SOLDIER *extends
the Red Zone.*
At some point, ADAM *finds a letter – addressed to* REEM *– on
the floor and picks it up.*

               Except the Palestinians don't come round
               very often cos the land isn't contested any
               more, it's been swallowed up.
               Things get lonely. And it's not much fun
               going dogging alone – in fact, it's not really
               dogging.
               It's public masturbation.
               The Intifada ended after Jawad's death. Not
               because of it, just chronologically that's what
               happened.
               It would be nice if Jawad bookended the
               Intifada, but he didn't.
               Things faded away, and then tensions with Iran
               shifted focus, and the Palestinians were worn
               down, so what else was going to happen?
               Anyway, the hundredth anniversary of Israel
               is right around the corner so that won't be
               peaceful.
               But for now it is

Bibi finally decomposed. His remains were
put in a huge mausoleum on Mount Hebron.
The West Bank borders shifted a bit.
We got some land, and they got
They didn't get much but the status quo was
maintained.
Not that anyone really cared.
It keeps on repeating itself and

REEM *enters, stands on the edge of the Red Zone –* ADAM
watches her.
As the Red Zone is extended, she has to keep stepping back.
Neither knows what to say.

ADAM	Hello?
REEM	Why are you. ADAM Why are you

Pause.

ADAM	Sorry.
REEM	No.
ADAM	You go.
REEM	Why are you here?
ADAM	I wanted to see if anyone else had survived.
REEM	Can I join you?
ADAM	Well I wouldn't but

REEM *steps into the Red Zone. Nothing happens.*

	Are you gonna mash my brain into hummus?
REEM	Maybe.
ADAM	–
REEM	How long before they turn on the searchlights, do you reckon?
ADAM	It won't be long.
REEM	So if you have a blender and some tahini we can end this quickly.
ADAM	–

REEM	I'm joking. This is where me and my husband used to come.
ADAM	So are you here because you want to… have sex… with me?
REEM	No. No, I don't want to do that. I don't want to do anything. I haven't done anything in a very long time.
ADAM	It was worth a try.
REEM	It wasn't. You've picked up some Arabic.
ADAM	I thought it'd be good.
REEM	Are you looking for a pat on the back?
ADAM	No.
REEM	Look, I don't know why you're here, Adam, but this is meant to be some kind of closure. Except having a conversation with you is the exact opposite of that, so I'd like you to leave.

ADAM *doesn't leave.*

	I have Sara's ID.
ADAM	What?
REEM	I found it. On the floor, near where Salwa was… And I don't really know what to do with it, I just have it. I hold on to it.
ADAM	Can I see it?

Slowly, REEM *hands it over.*

REEM	You can keep it if you like.
ADAM	Thank you. –
REEM	I met her.

ADAM   Excuse me?

REEM   Your daughter. I wish I hadn't but I met Sara.

ADAM   Oh.

REEM   It feels like maybe you should know.
            Like it feels important, or poignant, or
            something, that I met Sara and Sara met me.
            Except I don't really know what – she seemed
            nice, is all.

ADAM   She was nice.

Pause. Then ADAM *reaches into his pocket.*

            I'm meant to give you this in return. It's my
            prop for the scene.

ADAM *holds up a letter.* REEM *takes it. She looks at it, opens it.*

REEM   It's in English. It's from the playwright.

ADAM   What does he say?

REEM   He says:
            Hello Reem,
            I wanted to remind you that you don't exist.

REEM *checks that she's solid, that she does in fact exist.*

            You're not real. Or did you forget?
            You're a character, a cipher, just a way for me
            to make sense of all this.
            This… thing… that's happening a few
            thousand miles away on a patch of land that
            I've never even visited.
            I am Palestinian – I'm half-Palestinian – but
            I'm scared of visiting because people die
            there.
            People like Jawad. And Sayeed. And Sara.
            And Salwa. And Tariq. And Loubna.
            I'm sorry about them.
            People only pay attention when there's a high
            death count.
            And even when people do pay attention they
            still forget.

*I'm telling you this because you shouldn't get
your hopes up.*
This is fiction.
*So your story has to end, and usually when a
story ends it has a conclusion – but this one
doesn't.*
*You see, I've spent the last few years trying to
come up with a meaning, some kind of
purpose, for your story, what it all adds up to,
but I've got nothing.*
Sorry.
*All I know is this: my family had money. They
left Palestine in nineteen forty-eight and
never looked back.*
Your family didn't.
I can't even speak Arabic.
*Sure, I sometimes eat hummus – but so does
everyone else.*
I'm very middle class.
My skin is very white.
It makes me think I'm not Palestinian at all.
It makes me think my blood runs thin.
*Or maybe I am Palestinian but people always
give me a look when I say it – like they
assume Palestinians have to have brown skin
and throw rocks and plant bombs.*
Sometimes I'd prefer to be all white.
*Sometimes I like the cultural capital of being
Palestinian – like when I get money to write
a play.*
*The point is, I don't understand your world,
I don't understand you – and once this theatre
stops paying me to tell your story, I'll stop
telling it.*
That's what's happening now.
*And I'm sorry that I can't understand you –
not properly anyway – I just watch the news
every now and then and tell people 'Hmm,
yes, it's all very complicated, isn't it?'*
*Maybe, by the time you read this, there'll be a
Palestinian state – but I don't think it's likely.*

*Either way, you should know that I'm too lazy
to fight for one. I remember going on a march
in support of Palestine but didn't sign up for the
newsletter because I don't like getting spam.
That's who's writing this, and the truth is I
don't know what's going on: telling your story
didn't give me any answers so all that
happens now is things come to an end, we all
go home.*
I can't help that.
*And it's not happy or sad or anything in
particular. It's just an ending: a searchlight
turns on, a conversation ends, it's a mess.
And after it's done, we'll try not to forget you.
But in the end, none if this is real, none of this
is anything, and we'll simply move on.*

REEM *stops reading. They don't speak for a while.*

No they won't.

ADAM   What?

REEM   People aren't going to move on.

ADAM   They always do.

REEM   They won't because things don't end on
              anyone else's terms but mine.
              This is mine – no one forgets that.
              My name's Reem by the way, did you know
              that Adam?

ADAM *hesitates, looks at the audience.*

              Don't look at them, look at me, you didn't,
              did you – my name is Reem Hajri.
              And you know my son's name.

ADAM   Jawad.

REEM   Jawad, yes, because we all know Jawad's
              name.
              And we know Loubna's name, because that's
              how it started.

We know Sara's name.
And we know my name, and will *remember*
my name, because that's how it ends.
Reem Hajri.

REEM *holds out her hand.* ADAM *doesn't move, so* REEM
grabs him, roughly.

Tell me I'm not real: you can touch me, you
can feel me.

Then she turns to the audience.

Does anyone else want to tell me I'm not real?
Does anyone else want to tell me I don't
matter, that this is all fucked, and we should
just go home and forget about it?
Because I don't believe that.
Anyone?
–

I believe my story matters and you cannot
forget a story that matters.
And I believe things are a mess, but we can
still find answers if we care enough to
THINK.

A searchlight turns on.

No. Turn the searchlight off.

It stays on.

That's not what happens, turn it off. Turn it
OFF.

It stays on. REEM *stares into the light.*

Fine. So this is how it ends: a real ending.
The searchlight turns off.

But it doesn't.

The searchlight turns off, it does, and then
Reem, she, she
She makes sense of it all.
Of everything, she has answers, and she
tells us

There's a faint whistling – the sound of a rocket which gets louder, louder, louder, louder, louder.

> She does, she says
> She says

Then there's silence: we realise the rocket is about to strike.

> Oh shit.

Then there's a
Blackout.

A Nick Hern Book

two Palestinians go dogging first published in Great Britain in 2022 as a paperback original by Nick Hern Books Limited, The Glasshouse, 49a Goldhawk Road, London W12 8QP, in association with the Royal Court Theatre and Theatre Uncut

Cover image: The separation wall on Derech Hevron, Bethlehem, Palestine (Alvan Kranzer/Alamy)

Designed and typeset by Nick Hern Books, London
Printed in the UK by Mimeo Ltd, Huntingdon, Cambridgeshire PE29 6XX

A CIP catalogue record for this book is available from the British Library

ISBN 978 1 84842 885 0

www.nickhernbooks.co.uk

facebook.com/nickhernbooks

twitter.com/nickhernbooks